NAVIGATING
THE ROAD
TO COLLEGE

A Handbook for Parents

ISBN-10: 1460901746
EAN-13: 9781460901748

NAVIGATING THE ROAD TO COLLEGE

A Handbook for Parents

Kris Hintz

To my son, Eric,
the love of my life

Acknowledgements

I would like to acknowledge the friendship, creativity, insights, encouragement, inspiration, and advice of many individuals who have been instrumental in the launching of my college and career consulting practice and this book.

My husband, Brad Hintz; and son, Eric Hintz.

My sister, Karen Snider; my brother-in-law and workshop colleague, Al "Doc" Snider; and my nieces, Laura and Caroline Snider.

My in-laws and second parents, Charles and Helen "Nonnie" Hintz; my sister-in-law, Kim Hintz Armour; my brother-In-law, Greg Armour; and my nephews, Nathan and Jacob Armour.

My late parents, Salvatore and Anita Falsetta; and my late intergenerational friend, Bea Weiss.

My friend, colleague, and reference editor, Deborah Ernst.

Authors, journalists, psychologists, researchers and filmmakers whose work and ideas have stimulated my thinking: Lynn O'Shaughnessy; Vicki Abeles; Dr. William Damon; Melissa Clinedinst and David Hawkins; Dr. Steven R. Antonoff; Loren Pope; Carol Fishman Cohen and Vivian Steir Rabin; Dr. Barbara K. Hofer and Abigail Sullivan Moore; Professor Amy Chua; Dr. James Hillman; and Dr. James Hollis.

Friends and colleagues who have helped me as idea contributors, true believers, role models, mentors, service providers, enthusiastic referrers, and early clients who trusted my instincts as their guide:

Janice, Brian, Grace and Lily Gallick; Anita, Miguel, Marcelo, Daniel, and Alexandre Porto; MaryBeth, Bob, Bobby, Michelle, and Jack Napor; Cathy, Eric, Paul, Annie, and Tommy Batterman; Elizabeth, Randall, Christian, and Kathryn Hansen; Don Betterton; Gerald Stern; Deborah, Jeff, Kestin, and Leah Gussoff; Dr. Elizabeth Simonetti; Christine Lopez; Kathy Cirlincione; Caroline, Gary, Burton, John, and Chad Gildersleeve; Judy and Meredith Longthorne; Annette, Luke, Luke Matthew, and Scott Beshar; Michael and Amy Lawlor; Ellen Morgenstern and Nicole Ouzounis; Scherlyn and Alexandra Garney; Henry and Gloria Aaron; Valerie Paik and Amy Gideon; Barbara Stolz, Theresa Must, and Joe Galioto; Mike Shapiro and Melanie WIlson; Joanne Ainsworth; Penney Riegelman; Don Austin; Dr. Richard DiBianca; Karen Ferretti; Martha Santiuste; David Wish; Carole Barabander; Jeffrey Neikrie; and my continuing source of inspiration, the late Debbie Neikrie.

Table of Contents

I. My Story

I. My Story

My name is Kris. I grew up in New Jersey and I spend most of my time there now, when I am not in Tucson, Arizona. A few years ago, I started Position U 4 College LLC, a college admissions, graduate school and career consulting firm, based in Basking Ridge, New Jersey.

I usually get my background out of the way quickly so I can move on to getting acquainted with my young clients. So. I earned my BA in psychology from the University of Pennsylvania (1978), an MBA in marketing from the Wharton School (1980), and a master's in psychology from Columbia University Teachers College (1996) with a focus in career development. I recently completed a college counseling certificate with UCLA (2010).

I spent twelve years as a marketing brand management executive with Clorox in the San Francisco Bay Area, Quaker Oats in Chicago, Coca-Cola Foods in Houston, and Nabisco in New Jersey. I have been happily married for over thirty years to Brad Hintz, Sanford Bernstein's equity analyst for the securities industry. We have a wonderful son, Eric, who is an economics major at Emory University.

Eric came into our lives in 1990, when I was a business director of cookies at Nabisco (now Kraft), and Brad was managing director and treasurer at Morgan Stanley. I continued my career at Nabisco for two years after our son was born, and then decided to leave the paid workforce, seeking a more flexible occupation outside the corporate world.

Columbia's graduate program allowed me to explore organizational psychology with the possibility of perhaps returning to the corporate arena. It also afforded me the opportunity to explore career counseling and family systems psychology and their related trajectories.

After completing my graduate degree in psychology, I elected to stay home full time to raise our son. Like many professional women of my generation, I redirected my corporate training to serve as a school, church, and community volunteer. When Eric began middle school, I found more time to explore a wide spectrum of interests. My bucket list included: psychological counseling and personal coaching; cartoon illustration and acrylic landscape painting; acoustic guitar building; computer graphics and Web design; musical video montage making; and choral music, meditation, and spirituality.

I explored the pros and cons of perhaps becoming a psychotherapist, which had always been an appealing road not taken for me. My parents' deaths were watershed experiences that led me through a period of inner seeking, such that I became a certified grief counselor as well as a deeper human being. After much soul-searching, I emerged knowing that my calling was not psychotherapy, but guidance of young people on the edge of their adult journey.

When Eric went through the college admissions process, I became convinced that becoming a college admissions consultant would be a rewarding career that could integrate my marketing and psychology background in an ideal way. My corporate experience made it a natural extension for me to offer services in graduate school admissions and career coaching as well.

When Eric started at Emory University in 2008, I established Position U 4 College LLC. I am fortunate to have built a thriving client base and a meaningful, flexible career that allows me to help young people discover their distinctive strengths and find their way.

My office is in our seventy-year-old farmhouse in Basking Ridge, looking out on our rustic red barn and the lush English gardens that remind me of my mother and fill me with daily gratitude for life's blessings. Our ten-year-old Sheltie, Angel, border collie puppy, Penny, and black cat on his eighth life, Mr. Pud, permit me to meet with my young clients as long as I don't neglect their dinner.

It was great fun designing my company's logo and co-creating its Web site[1], without having to gain approval from anyone "important " back in the corporate world. During that first year, I launched two blogs, collegeblog[2] for parents of high school students and careerblog[3] for college students and recent college graduates.

Having stumbled upon blogging as a natural outgrowth of building a reputation in my field, I soon discovered that offering perspectives to my fellow parents on raising adolescents was a special calling in its own right. Friends and clients asked if I would publish a collection of my most popular blog posts, or "essays," as a college consultant would say. Their encouragement led to the creation of this book.

II. My Perspective

1. Honorable Adulthood

*God willing, we might still have lived and loved together, and see
our boys grown up to honorable manhood around us.*

– Sullivan Ballou,
Nineteenth C. US army major

September 1990. Our only son, Eric, was six months old. My
husband, Brad, and I became deeply engrossed in Ken Burns'
PBS documentary, *The Civil War*[1], whenever Eric would miracu-
lously fall asleep. We were just getting used to the awkward
new idea of parenthood, with no clue as to where this strange
new odyssey might take us.

Brad knows all Civil War battles by heart, a casualty of what I call
the 1865 Male Chromosome. But the film's compelling archival
photographs, brought alive by the "Ken Burns effect" and Jay
Unger's haunting fiddle composition, "Ashoken Farewell,"[2] guaranteed that I would be mesmerized by the masterpiece as well.

We were both captivated by the touching legendary letter of
Union Major Sullivan Ballou, written to his wife before being
mortally wounded in the First Battle of Bull Run. The letter's
most memorable words were, for us: *"God willing, we might still
have lived and loved together, and see our boys grown up to honorable manhood around us."*[3]

Our son will turn twenty-one in a few months. He is successful
by any standard, a junior at Emory University with fine academic performance. But so many years ago, while listening to that

eloquent letter, its immortal words echoing across time from a distant century, we had tacitly agreed to our own unique touchstone for parental success.

Our vision was that our son would grow to *honorable manhood*, a phrase that embodies character, independence, and purpose. I am proud to say that our son has developed these admirable qualities in abundance.

As a college consultant, I meet parents with all sorts of goals for their high school students. Parental goals for their offspring have included: an Ivy League education; a college diploma, period, with minimal debt; a college major that can generate a secure living; settling down and raising a family on the same coast as the parents' home; self-actualization that has eluded the parents; a career that surpasses the parents' accomplishments; surviving the recessionary economy; or just being "happy." The list goes on. Sometimes it is hard to determine what results qualify as a success.

I've encountered my share of evolved and inspiring parents, as well as occasional misguided ones. We've all met (and occasionally been) helicopter parents[4] who discourage their teens' bid for autonomy, ignoring Robert Heinlein's sage advice: *"Don't handicap your children by making their lives easy."*[5]

At the other end of the spectrum, we have all known parents so absorbed in their own concerns that their kids practically have to raise themselves. They are perhaps following in the footsteps of comedian Roseanne Barr, who quipped: *"I figure that if the children are alive when I get home, I've done my job."*[6]

I am certainly in no position to judge anyone else, with my own humbling missteps never far from my mind. What I prefer to offer is supportive wisdom from Major Ballou, that loving husband and insightful father from the nineteenth century, whose moving words have given us so much direction in the past twenty-one years.

Honorable Adulthood. To me, *honorable* means behaving with honesty, fairness, empathy, and integrity, consistent with one's beliefs and values. *Adulthood* connotes independence, inner-directedness, self-sufficiency, and maturity. It is challenging for any young person to achieve, an ever-moving target. It can also be bittersweet for parents to release their precious offspring to the uncontrollable terrain of their own autonomy. But isn't that what we have always desired for our children, from the very beginning?

This paradigm can give you guidance throughout your children's adolescence. If you are tempted to fight your kids' battles, micromanage their college essays, squelch their youthful idealism, pressure them into a school choice, major, or career that allays your own anxieties and addresses your unmet aspirations, yet drains them of genuine ownership, voice, and meaning, think again. *Are you encouraging honorable adulthood?*

2. What Is Important to Colleges? Top Ten Factors

Things which matter most must never be at the mercy of things which matter least.

–Johann Wolfgang von Goethe,
Eighteenth C. German writer and polymath

SATs as an extracurricular activity? Traveling soccer clubs beginning in kindergarten? Making peanut butter and jelly sandwiches for the homeless? President of the tiddlywink club? *What's most important to colleges, anyway?*

The National Association of College Admission Counseling (NACAC) offers guidance on this crucial question. Based on Admission Trends Surveys 1993–2009 from the *NACAC State of College Admission 2010 Report*[1], I can suggest ten priorities for your high school student:

1. Grades in college prep (87 percent). It makes sense that grades in college preparatory "solids" (math, science, history, English, foreign language) would be "number one." In NACAC's survey, this factor drew the highest percentage (87 percent) of colleges and universities attributing "considerable importance" to its impact in admission decisions. Grades are a "cross country run" while test results are a "sprint." Across four years, grades show a student's "true colors," not only the smarts, but also the work ethic, discipline, and ability to deliver over the long haul.

2. Strength of curriculum (71 percent). Straight As are great, but is your student enrolled in honors, AP (Advanced Placement), or IB (International Baccalaureate) courses? Colleges want students that seek to challenge themselves. High schools' advanced course options vary widely, but admissions officers want to see that your teen took advantage of the offerings in the school he or she attended.

It's a two-edged sword. Some elite high schools with splendid AP offerings raise the bar for entry so high that above-average students have little access. Late bloomers cannot "jump on the train" halfway through high school. Parents need to be aware of the curriculum from eighth grade on, and encourage their student to "board the train" (consistent with aptitude) before it "leaves the station."

The $64,000 question: "Is it better to get an A in a regular course, or a B in honors?" Wiseacre answer: *"A in an honors course!"* But seriously, a student who excels at a specific subject, should be in the honors section of that course. "All honors" is not necessary, but "at least a few" is advisable.

3. Admissions test scores (58 percent). Test scores are the "sprint," but they are still significant, let's not kid ourselves. Yes, many colleges are now test optional. But particularly if your kid applies to large state schools, expect standardized tests to play a key role. Public universities claim to be shifting toward holistic admissions, but that labor-intensive shift will not happen overnight. In chapter three, I will examine the relative admissions decision impact of all these factors in public versus private institutions.

If you suspect your child has a learning challenge that may require testing accommodations such as extra time, *address it early.* Using our "sprint" analogy, don't insist that your child heroically leap over hurdles in the race that others don't have, to be "treated like everybody else." Maybe your child *isn't like everybody else.*

4. Grades in all courses (46 percent). Grades in electives count too, especially if electives are in subject areas in which your student plans to major.

5. Essays (26 percent). The importance of essays varies by the type of institution: a small test-optional liberal arts college weighs essays more heavily than a large state university, as we will discuss in detail in chapter three. That said, in 2009, more than a fourth of all colleges and universities viewed essays as a factor of "considerable importance." That percentage has doubled since 1993. *So ace that personal statement!*

6. Demonstrated interest (21 percent). This factor has tripled since the first time it was measured in 2003. *Demonstrated interest*, as evidenced by campus visits, attendance at admissions road shows, and knowledge about the school in applicant essays, has become a hot button for admissions people required to maximize their yield.

7. Teacher recommendation (17 percent). Beyond earning good grades, it is imperative to be more than just a number in one's class. Your student needs to create a relationship with at least a few teachers during high school, especially junior year. Gaining personal credibility with teachers is not just essential for recommendations; it is a modus operandi that will help your young adult become successful in any future field.

8. Counselor recommendation (17 percent). The guidance counselor not only writes the cornerstone recommendation for each applicant; he or she is the spokesperson for the applicant with every college. Therefore, if your teen attends a large high school where it is hard for counselors to get to know students, your student must get to the guidance office whenever possible all four years, and keep the counselor informed about achievements and issues. Foster your student's life skill of building personal equity with administrators, to the degree possible, even in a large pool of students.

9. Class rank (16 percent). Some high schools downplay (or do not publish) class rank data to dial down competitive attitudes. But you know vaguely where your student is, and you may be able to at least get decile or quintile information. This factor can help gauge how realistic your student's target colleges are.

10. Extracurricular activities (9 percent). So this is where all the hours of playing varsity sports and rehearsing for the winter musical goes, at the *BOTTOM* of the top ten factors?

Yes. So, unless your child is a Division I athlete or a classical violin prodigy bound for Julliard, extracurricular activities should be undertaken for personal development and fun. Not as an "ace in the hole" for university acceptance! College is an *academic institution*, which is why, on the NACAC list, grades are at the top and activities are at the bottom.

3. Public versus Private Universities or Liberal Arts Colleges

A university is what a college becomes when the faculty loses interest in the students.

–John Ciardi,
American poet, translator, and etymologist

I ask my clients early on if they wish to consider public or private universities or liberal arts colleges. Students usually give me a blank stare. Parents either recoil in horror if they are already convinced that Ivies are the only acceptable choice, or they brighten with relief that they may be able to steer their kid to a Big Ten school and afford retirement.

There are many other distinctions between these three types of institutions besides cost, so let me enlighten you:

1. Public universities. In the U.S., most public institutions are state universities, founded and operated by state governments. Every state has at least one public university. This is partially due to the 1862 Morrill Land-Grant Acts, which gave each eligible state 30,000 acres of federal land to sell to finance public institutions offering study for practical fields in addition to the liberal arts. Many public universities began as teacher training schools and eventually were expanded into comprehensive universities.[1]

2. Private universities. Many U.S. universities and colleges are private, operated as educational and research non-profit organizations. The term "university" is primarily used to designate graduate education and research institutions.[2]

3. Liberal arts colleges. The *Encylopaedia Britannica Concise* offers a definition of the *liberal arts* as a "college or university curriculum aimed at imparting general knowledge and developing general intellectual capacities, in contrast to a professional, vocational, or technical curriculum."[3] The contemporary liberal arts include literature, languages, philosophy, history, mathematics, and science. While most liberal arts colleges are private, there are some public liberal arts schools as well.[4]

Private versus public: Cost. It is general knowledge that public university tuition is less expensive for in-state students than out-of-state students. Public tuition, even for out-of-state students, is far less expensive than tuition for students at private institutions.

For example, the 2010-11 tuition and fees for an in-state student at the State University of New York Binghamton is $4,970 per year, and for an out-of-state student, $13,380; Kiplinger's ranks Binghamton as the top U.S. out-of-state public school value.[5] With room and board of $11,886, the annual attendance cost for an in-state student is $18, 825. SUNY's smart marketers compare these costs to a private university, with tuition and fees at $39,150, room and board $12,000, and an annual cost of attendance $51,150.[6]

Private versus public: Academic quality and the undergraduate experience. Is there an educational quality trade-off between public and private universities?

Public universities figure prominently in *U.S. News & World Report*'s 2011 rankings of the top fifty national universities.[7] These rankings are based on seven broad categories of academic quality: peer assessment; retention and graduation of students; faculty resources; student selectivity; financial resources; alumni giving; graduation rate performance; and high school counselor ratings.

The public universities in the top fifty national universities include UC Berkeley, UCLA, U Virginia, U Michigan, UNC Chapel Hill, William & Mary, Georgia Tech, UC San Diego, UC Davis, UC Santa Barbara, UC Irvine, U Washington, U Texas Austin, U Wisconsin Madison, Penn State, and U Illinois Urbana-Champaign.

However, attending a public university will require trade-offs in the quality of the undergraduate experience, such as *larger class sizes*. Public institutions in the top fifty have a percentage of classes with fewer than twenty students ranging from 30 to 60 percent. For perspective, private institutions in the top fifty have a percentage of classes with fewer than twenty students ranging from 47 to 80 percent.

University versus liberal arts college undergraduate experience. Generally, a university is a good choice for pursuing a field that is centered in its own professional school, such as engineering, business, or nursing. However, a university is by definition a research institution, so the faculty focus will be on research, not teaching undergrads. The "publish or perish" phenomenon and its unfortunate impact on the undergraduate experience is insightfully articulated in *Academically Adrift: Limited Learning on College Campuses* by Richard Alum and Josipa Roksa. [8]

Class size is likely to be somewhat larger in a university setting (even in a private institution). The *U.S. News & World Report's* 2011[9] rankings show that privates in the top fifty national universities have a percentage of classes with fewer than twenty students ranging from 47 to 80 percent, versus 57 to 96 percent for the top fifty national liberal arts colleges.

Differences in the admissions process for public versus private insitutions. Based on Admission Trends Surveys 1993–2009 from the *NACAC State of College Admission 2010 Report,* I will describe the relative differences in public versus private institutions attributing "considerable importance" in the admissions decision to the ten factors cited in chapter two.[10]

Grades and test scores were the key factors in both types of institutions, but there were relative differences. *GPA in college prep courses* was viewed as having "considerable importance" in admissions decisions by 85 percent of private versus 90 percent of public institutions. *Strength of curriculum* was important to 69 percent of privates versus 75 percent of publics. *Admissions testing* was important to 54 percent of privates versus 71 percent of publics. *Grades in all courses* was important to 44 percent of privates versus 52 percent of publics.

Given the huge number of applicants versus admissions staff in public universities, it makes sense that quantitative measures of achievement were cited as of "considerable importance" more in publics versus privates. Public universities' intention to shift to more holistic admissions may not be realistic due to the applicant number versus admissions staff imbalance. In contrast, most schools that have joined the "test optional" movement are private.

Private institutions placed more importance on the *essay* (31 versus 13 percent in public universities); *extra-curricular activities* (10 versus 5 percent); *portfolio* (10 versus 5 percent); *interview* (9 versus 0 percent); and *AP or IB tests* (9 versus 2 percent). Generally, privates placed more importance on qualitative measures that are more labor-intensive to assess.

So there are plenty of differences between public and private institutions, and also between universities and liberal arts colleges. The decision of which of these three paths to take is a fundamental one that will deeply impact your young adult's undergraduate experience.

4. Do You Need a "Passion" to Get into College?

Action expresses priorities.

−Mohandas Gandhi,
Indian independence leader

Who brought that ubiquitous word **"PASSION"** to the college admissions process? Consultants? "How To Apply" books? Admissions officers? Guidance counselors?

This word does not come from a teen vocabulary. It's too extreme, too emotional, too revealing, too blurred with sex or romance, too intense, too uncool, too hokey. It's a buzzword of the college admissions industry, designed to market students to colleges. Some high school students appear to have that unique focus in high school. But most students would probably not authentically describe themselves as "passionate."

What is an admissions officer looking for that we call "passion"? I found a clue in an Urban Dictionary definition: *"Passion is when you put more energy into something than is required to do it. It is more than just enthusiasm or excitement, passion is ambition that is materialized into action to put as much heart, mind, body, and soul into something as is possible."*[1]

So how do you know if your kids have passion?

1. How do they spend most of their extracurricular time?
Parents can muddy the waters. Many parents believe their kids must be involved in multiple activities: sports, performing arts,

community service. But admissions professionals send a consistent message that *colleges want depth rather than breadth.*

So it is better for your student to do one extracurricular activity at a deep level than to be a jack-of-all-trades, master of none. Some parents feel apologetic about that. But I'd rather see a young person do one service project that demands commitment, like Eagle Scout or Girl Scout Gold, instead of food pantries or book drives that require only casual, occasional involvement.

The Common Application asks the applicant to list key activities, with level of leadership, years of participation, and hours/week and weeks/year spent on the activity. Why? Colleges want to see *how much time the applicant actually spends* on each pursuit: *a concrete measure of dedication!*

2. How do they spend their truly free time? My niece, Laura, is exceptionally talented in the performing arts. Throughout high school she spent her formal extracurricular time in choral, orchestra, dance, and theater groups. However, in her rare "spare time," she wrote stories. It is not surprising that creative writing is now her major in college.

Often a teenager's spare time pleasures can be observed from early childhood. Have you ever heard a civil engineer's family talk about how she always loved to build with Legos® or an attorney's family recall his childhood mastery of Scrabble®?

A parent's observations, filed away for years, can be selectively retrieved as clues to an unfolding mystery, when a high school student feels at a loss about what he might want to explore in college. Such contributions must be rare, humble recollections only, seeds planted without any hidden agenda, respecting the adolescent's right to accept or reject any suggestions.

3. In what school subjects do they excel? On what school projects do they seem to spend the most time? I'm not talking about remedial catch-up in difficult courses. I mean enthusiastic, curious, creative "go the second mile" involvement. It's all about putting in *more energy than what is required*. Some students become so excited by a subject they will actually debate issues with parents or siblings at home. For less outgoing students, you may need to ask probing questions or heighten your observational powers to detect signs of passion.

When students don't seem to be particularly turned on by any subject, it may be worthwhile to find a more stimulating learning environment (a seminar-style or hands-on class). They also may need exposure to more topics and experiences to find out more about what they really like. Academic clubs and teams or an explorative summer camp program also might draw them out.

Passion doesn't need to be outwardly expressed. Every human being is a puzzle. Guiding young people to discover their passions, and finding colleges that will nurture those interests, is an art that requires open-minded listening and insightful observation.

Self-discovery is a long, circuitous process that continues for years beyond high school. (We are still doing it, aren't we?) Colleges don't require students to commit to a major or career choice on applications. Premature pigeonholing is not the goal here, just helping a young person find pursuits that genuinely resonate.

I recall a bright, accomplished student with a reserved style who was attempting to wrap up our session quickly one evening in October, several years ago. As I blabbed on about the essay, he quietly rose to his feet and said, "Don't want to miss the Yankees."

With no fanfare, his passion was announced, offering a subtle clue that this would be a significant element in his college selection process. Sure enough, he now attends the University of Michigan, where excellent academics and spectator sports go hand in hand.

5. Your Target Colleges–And It's a Moving Target

When you aim for perfection, you discover it's a moving target.

–George Fischer,
American education activist

The big college admissions headline in spring, 2010, was the increased number of students on waiting lists for highly selective colleges, as exemplified by the *New York Times* article "Top Colleges Have Bigger Waiting Lists"[1] and the *Washington Post* article "College Wait Lists Grow as Schools Hedge Bets on Enrollment Numbers."[2]

It's not that hard to figure out, really. The baby boomers had kids, leading to a huge population explosion. The online Common Application made it easy to apply to more schools than ever before. In simple economic terms, demand for spaces in highly selective colleges grew, but supply remained fixed.

So it is harder to get into a prestigious college than it was several decades ago. Parents are usually shocked when told by guidance counselors that the university they attended is a "reach" for their own children. It contradicts the Horatio Alger wisdom that says you work hard and make sacrifices so that your offspring can someday do better than you.

Once families accept that harsh reality, there is an even more elusive one that may blindside them. The new "rules" of who-gets-into-where are *fluid*. Applications continue to increase. Some schools are better than others at grabbing market share of the ever-growing number of applications.

In spring, 2010, *US News and World Report*[3] asked experts to identify institutions in each ranking category that are making the most promising and innovative changes in the areas of academics, faculty, and student life. Some schools may be unfamiliar, while some are household names. The top ten "up-and-coming" national universities (with ties) include: U Maryland Baltimore County, Arizona State, Drexel, Northeastern, George Mason, Indiana-Purdue Indianapolis, U Central Florida, U Delaware, Clemson, and Wake Forest. The top ten "up-and-coming" liberal arts colleges (with ties) include: Hendrix, Ursinus, College of St. Benedict, Whitman, UNC Asheville, Agnes Scott, Roanoke, U Richmond, Calvin, Washington and Williamette.

So it's a moving target. Schools that may have been spot-on for your student back when you were applying to college have no relevance today. *Sorry, it's ancient history.* But even the schools that would have been on-target for your kid five years ago, when an older sibling or cousin was applying to school, may be irrelevant as well. *It's a **real** moving target.*

So, does this mean that any recent historical acceptance information can't be used to gauge your student's chances? No, but take it all with a grain of salt. If the school was realistic for your student even last year, but it's a "hot" school gaining in popularity, your teen could just miss by a hair this year and be wait- listed.

To hedge their bets on that possibility, I advise applicants to apply to more schools clustered in the target "realistic" zone, as well as more schools slightly below that level in selectivity. Most students tend to apply to too many "far reach" and "very likely" schools, *but not enough in between,* in the *target zone* or slightly below (this is the single most common and dangerous mistake college applicants make today, in my opinion). It is human nature to swing for the bleachers, but having too many "Hail Mary Pass" schools is a waste of energy that could be better spent on more realistic options. Safeties your child could never *really* picture attending are a waste of time as well.

If students' lists are filled with "Hail Marys" and super safes, it may *appear* that they are applying to "enough" schools, but *they actually are not*. They could be disappointed by ending up on waiting lists and ultimately enrolling at colleges that will be "OK," but where they may feel not sufficiently stimulated by peers. After all the effort and money we spend on college, shouldn't it be a satisfying experience?

Is it a compromise to manage our teens' expectations a little lower than the lofty institutions we may have always dreamed our offspring would attend? No, it is our responsibility as parents to prepare them for the world *they* are entering, not the world we lived in. It behooves us to do our homework before setting college expectations. We owe it to them to check our naive pipe dreams–and egos—at the door when we start the college process.

So if you believe your son or daughter should apply to Princeton, do a little research before booking a night at the Nassau Inn. What does it take to get into Princeton today? Recently, I attended the commencement exercises at a preeminent New Jersey public high school. When the Princeton-bound valedictorian spoke, I was literally blown away by his background. Besides having the requisite perfect GPA and SAT scores, this young man was an All-State violinist, had conducted laboratory cancer research, and held (*of course!*) an advanced degree black belt in karate.

Is it fair to influence one's child to set sights so high, unless you are in touch what it *truly* requires today? Sometimes parents are crestfallen when I seem to be steering their student toward "under-Ivies." I feel like a dream stealer, dashing hopes that parents have held for many years, whether they attended an elite institution themselves or are hard working immigrants with high aspirations for the next generation. To offer my clients perspective,

I say, "I don't know if I could get into my own alma mater, the University of Pennsylvania, if I were applying today."

The good news: just as the Ivies aren't the same as they were decades ago, neither are the schools that your guidance counselor or college consultant may recommend for your student. This evolution is only partially driven by the crowding out of high-caliber students at Ivies. The most ambitious colleges, like aggressive companies, adopt competitive growth strategies to become the "go to" schools for these strong applicants.

For example, over the past few decades, the University of Southern California has been driving a meteoric rise through strategic investment of endowment funding in state-of-the-art facilities, academic talent, and leading-edge research. Elon University, decades ago a regional North Carolina college of moderate reputation, transformed itself into an Eastern Seaboard phenomenon through a brilliant, well-financed repositioning strategy.[4] Hendrix, Agnes Scott, and Ursinus gained publicity when "discovered" by Loren Pope, author of *Colleges That Change Lives*[5], attracting an increasingly higher-quality student body.

Moreover, the student caliber at competitive "under-Ivy" schools is significantly higher than you would have expected decades ago. Simply put, today there isn't room for all high-achieving kids in just a handful of schools. They have to go somewhere, and *they do*. Think of it as a huge recalibration.

So aim high, but accurately.

6. Everybody Needs a Tiger

*A hundred years from now...it will not matter what
my bank account was, the sort of house I lived in, or the
kind of car I drove...but the world may be different because
I was important in the life of a child.*

–Kathy Davis,
American feminist scholar

Amy Chua's controversial memoir, *The Battle Hymn of the Tiger Mother*[1], has created a viral media firestorm. I personally welcome any provocative book that elicits strong feelings, prompting thoughtful conversation about raising our children. Let me share a reflection on this bestelling book that I believe will have universal resonance.

Everybody needs a "Tiger."

No, I don't mean that everyone needs a Chinese mother with a harsh, verbally abusive style. That's the side of the iconoclastic Yale law professor that we'd all prefer to jettison; in retrospect, she probably would too.

But wait; let's not throw the baby out with the proverbial bath water. What *worked* in Amy Chua's Eastern parenting approach, and what can we all learn from it?

The secret of the Eastern formula's success, in my view, is the *power of one-on-one*. It's the power of having an *adult champion*. Every child can benefit from having a *passionate tutor* who believes in the child, works one-on-one, pushes the child to do his or her best, will not give up on the child, and will not let the child give up on him or herself.

We need to look no further than *The Miracle Worker*[2] for proof of the life-changing power of one-on-one. The intensely devoted tutor, Anne Sullivan Macy, unlocked the power of language for deaf, blind prodigy Helen Keller over a century ago. As a child, I was awestruck by the persevering tough love portrayed by Anne Bancroft's "Teacher" in the Oscar-winning 1962 film, resulting in Patty Duke's "Helen" spelling her first word, W-A-T-E-R, at the pump house.

So the Tiger does *not* have to be a mother, an issue raised by Carol Fishman Cohen in her recent *Working Mother* article, "Asian-Style Parenting Means Mom Stays Home."[3] I can think of multiple examples in my own family, and I presume you can too.

My husband, Brad, tells the story of his paternal Swedish grandmother, who read to him constantly when he was little, fueling his lifelong love of books. When I was a corporate executive, we hired a Brooklyn Jewish grandmother as a nanny, Bea, who did the same for our son.

In high school, I was the persistent AP US History quizzer, but it was Brad who registered to take SAT II US History along with Eric on a $50 bet. Who won? That's confidential, but *they both nailed it!*

Like Secretary of State Hillary Rodham Clinton, I believe that *It Takes a Village*[4] to raise a child. My version is a village of one-on-one relationships with *charismatic adults,* a term coined by Dr. Robert Brooks in *Raising Resilient Children: Fostering Strength, Hope and Optimism in Your Child.*[5]

Dr. Brooks explains: "In numerous studies, when resilient adults were asked what they considered to be of most importance in assisting them to overcome adversity in their childhood, invariably the first response was 'someone who believed in me and stood by me.'"[6]

Beyond extended family, these charismatic adults included, for my son: music instructors, tutors, camp counselors, sports coaches, academic teachers, and a martial arts *Sensei* who formed a special relationship with him. Each adult brings his or her own unique gift to a young person's life. *I believe every kid should have as many Tigers as possible!*

When I decided to become a college coach, I hoped to "pay it forward" to say thank you to charismatic adults who championed me when I was growing up, as well as the Tigers who influenced our son. In my practice and pro bono work, I get to play a rewarding third party role in guiding an adolescent's self-discovery process, influencing a teen's trajectory toward college and career.

I love being somebody's *Tiger!*

7. A College Consultant's Grown-Up Christmas List

No more lives torn apart, that wars would never start, and time would heal all hearts…This is my grown-up Christmas list.

–Written by D. Foster, L .T. Jenner, A. Grant,
Performed by Amy Grant, American singer-songwriter

Amy Grant's touching rendition of "Grown-Up Christmas List"[1] was omnipresent on the car radio this season. I welcomed it, far more than the slaphappy holiday fare that glosses over the complex lives we all lead, textured with joy and pain, gain and loss, peace laced with worry and uncertainty. No holiday is as pure and simple as the songs portray it.

I share my students' anxieties and disappointments as well as joys, and December is a bittersweet time. While many seniors are accepted Early Decision or Early Action, some are not. When early applications are deferred or denied, the sting is especially painful.

In *Admission Matters: What Students and Parents Need to Know about Getting into College* [2], December heartbreak is vividly described: "The problem with an early application denial is that it usually occurs in isolation, and also at holiday time…students usually apply early to only one college, and those who receive denials have no simultaneous acceptances to ease the blow."[3]

But acceptance stress is only one kind of trial that high school seniors face in December. So here is *my* grown-up Christmas list:

1. I wish students and families were free to separate a young person's self-esteem from acceptance at a specific school. There is a suitable higher education choice for every individual. Our society is preoccupied with prestige, symbolized by material wealth or college pedigree.

But it is unrealistic to expect that "baby boomlet" children of "boomer" parents who graduated from elite colleges can all get into those same schools today (i.e., growing demand vs. static supply). Even academic stars will face rejection unless they adjust expectations. There are only eight Ivies, but 2,500 four-year institutions[4] in the USA: your kid has *got to* get in somewhere!

As a separate issue, many kids do not possess interests or skills that fit with four-year schools. But they also have plenty of choices, among 1,700 two-year schools[5] that are more focused on applied career training. Despite our culture's disdain for what we used to call *vocational* education, many kids would be happier, and more likely to get jobs in this economy, if they learned medical technology instead of archaeology. With apologies to Indiana Jones, how many archaeologists *do we really need?*

Look, if everyone decides to go to the same restaurant the same night, someone is bound to be disappointed. No reason to lose self-esteem over it: it's simply supply and demand. If we truly understood that, the college process would be more about discovering one's unique "fit," and less about "getting in." I wish parents could gear their kids to find a school where they'd thrive and find their way, without a feeling of failure if rejected by a "hot" school that is probably not a good match anyway.

2. I wish students would start preparing for college earlier. *WHAT?* you say. *It's already stressful enough, starting spring of junior year.* Hold on! I don't mean taking the SATs in kindergarten or visiting campuses in utero. I mean, simply *thinking about the* *future.* Young athletes know all about their physical capabilities and improvements they can make to switch to a more desirable position or team. But when I ask some student athletes about their academic abilities, or what they imagine doing for a living someday, I get a blank stare...

Not that an adolescent should have this all worked out now, but it would be nice to at least have a clue. Only in the USA is it acceptable to apply to college "undeclared." Why are European teens able to pick an occupational focus but Americans are not?

At minimum, a student can prepare by earning good grades. All colleges want that, even if the applicant doesn't know what he or she wants to be when grown up. So my second wish is that parents would urge their students to start preparing for a future through focused, earnest academic performance--early.

3. I wish standardized tests were not timed. We often hear about time accommodation for learning disabilities, or LDs. Do more kids have LD's today than back in the Fifties? Are they just more frequently diagnosed? Or, as simplistic cynics insist on cruelly proposing, is LD just an excuse for poor motivation? My instinct says, when a problem is epidemic, there's a broad-based cause. But I doubt the answer is that every American suddenly just decided to become lazy. Someday scientists may figure out that learning disabilities are linked to environmental toxins, food supply, or another ubiquitous force that has only become prevalent in the past fifty years.

Meanwhile, the movement to obtain LD extra time accommodations has unearthed a concern that was *always* there for some students: *paralyzing test anxiety.* Someday we may learn that families who go to great lengths to obtain accommodations were actually trying to help a kid with severe test anxiety.

If tests were not timed, LD students could demonstrate their true potential without jumping through bureaucratic hoops. Untimed testing could also measure the true potential of a much broader sector of students, those who suffer from test anxiety. (Please don't tell me how impractical this is: after all, it's just my Christmas wish.)

My guess is, there is one group of test-takers, high academic/low anxiety, who excel, timed or not. Another group, low academic/ low anxiety, test poorly, timed or not. But two groups, high academic/high anxiety and low academic/high anxiety, may do significantly better if *not* timed. *Non-timed tests would measure the true potential of these students.*

A 1995 study by Onwuegbuzie & Seaman, "The Effect of Time Constraints and Statistics Test Anxiety on Test Performance in a Statistics Course," concluded: "Both low- and high-anxious students performed better...under the untimed condition...However, *the benefit of the untimed examination was greater for high-anxious students than for low-anxious students.*"[6]

But they need to test your ability to think under pressure, don't they? Why? If you aspire to become MacGyver, diffusing bombs while seconds tick away, then timed testing is a good predictor of career success. But as a marketing executive, I *never* had to make a decision with a stopwatch ticking. *So what's the point of a timed test?*

I was one of those nervous test takers. It is amazing how I managed to get three Ivy League degrees, because I choked on the SATs, GREs and GMATs. My scores weren't disastrous, but they always *under* predicted my higher education performance.

If test stress is a cause of underestimation of college success in the population at large, it will be worse among economically disadvantaged groups without the luxury of paid tutors to help them practice under timed conditions. If "leveling the playing field" was the original purpose of standardized testing, this is one more dimension in which the wealthy win and the less affluent lose.

I have often comforted a client who earns excellent grades, yet cannot overcome test anxiety. But recently, in a pro bono setting, a terrific young woman from the inner city, a hard-working student with fine grades, was denied at a school due to low test scores. She had studied a workbook (tutoring was out of the question financially), but her scores were still too low. "Do you get nervous taking the SATs?" I asked. Fighting back tears, she nodded. "I always did too," I said.

That's why this is my third grown-up Christmas wish.

8. College Consultants? Who Needs 'em?

Good counselors lack no clients.

—William Shakespeare,
Sixteenth C. English playwright and poet

The current economy permits few luxuries. Why should families hire an independent college admissions consultant?

1. Focused one-on-one attention. In the middle of this decade, studies by the US Department of Education[1] and the National Association for College Admission Counseling[2] pointed to average public school counselor-to-student ratios in the range of 300–500 to 1. Guidance counselors can only devote part of their time to college advising, since their duties often include scheduling and discipline issues.

These hard working professionals are doing their best in a difficult situation. But for families who would like more individual attention for their high school student, an independent consultant can play a helpful role. I am a big believer in the power of one-to-one coaching.

2. Rising college competitiveness. *Admission Matters: What Students and Parents Need to Know about Getting into College* [3] identifies three factors that have made the college process more competitive and stressful than "back in the day": the "echo" boom (or baby boomlet), social changes, and the Internet.

The authors describe the demographic explosion that causes students to be "edged out" of top colleges at which their parents were accepted—supply and demand. "More high school graduates than ever are competing for seats in the freshman class...in 1997, there were 2.6 million graduates. By 2009, the number of high school graduates had grown to 3.3 million...they are projected to stay at or above 3.2 million at least until 2022."[4]

Social changes have increased the complexity and competitiveness of the process. "Application numbers have grown much faster than the age cohort...Not only are there more students graduating from high school each year, proportionally more of them want to go to college...At the same time, colleges themselves have increased their efforts to attract large, diverse pools of applicants."[5]

The Internet intensifies competition as well. Students can research schools efficiently, and online applications, such as the Common Application, have made it easy to apply to multiple colleges.[6]

This competitive, complex landscape requires more guidance than in the past. It can be misleading and unrealistic (and unfair to the child) to rely on parental historical benchmarks: "I went to Georgetown and my son is as smart as I am, so why shouldn't he be accepted?" A consultant can provide an updated perspective and insight into the rules of the new game.

3. Mistakes are costly. I am talking about cost in terms of student self-esteem as well as time and money. It is vital to have a realistic college list, with an appropriate number of "target" schools, not too many reaches or safes.

Unrealistic expectations may exacerbate the stress of the college process, and result in your teen having to "settle" for a school that is not the best fit. They say, "You can always transfer," and that's true. But having to start over at a new campus can be an emotional struggle.

And don't forget, transfer students are not always considered for scholarships for which freshmen are eligible. If the new college's requirements differ from those of the original school, the student may have to spend extra time and money taking additional courses. Why let your student go through this potentially costly "guinea pig" experience? Advice from an experienced counselor can prevent unnecessary expenditures of time, money, and angst.

You are about to shell out as much as $200K (for a private college), *one of the largest investments you will ever make.* An initial advisory service seems like a reasonable course of action before launching into such a venture.

4. A third party can help navigate the tricky parent-teen relationship. The college process creates the perfect storm in an already tense parent-teen dynamic. Your teen is seeking autonomy, trying to find his or her authentic voice, while you are seeking to protect your evolving young adult from disastrous consequences of high-risk behaviors. A third-party mentor can lower the tension. *Often a teenager is more willing to listen to a third party than to parents!*

5. An independent college consultant can help broaden opportunities for your student. A seasoned consultant has knowledge of many schools of which you may not be aware. A consultant has experience with resources to assist you in efficiently finding schools with strengths in your child's fields of interest, or "great fits" with your child's personality and social style.

Experienced consultants will be acquainted with excellent summer, gap year, and study abroad programs. Although most college consultants are not financial aid advisers per se, they are familiar with the process and can identify specialists. They also can put you in touch with tutors for standardized testing and even educational consultants for learning disabilities.

For information on choosing a consultant, check with the National Association for College Admission Counseling (NACAC) or the Independent Educational Consultants Association (IECA). Anyone you consider should be a member of one of these organizations and have a background in counseling, school guidance, or admissions. Other credentials include the IECA Training Institute or college counseling certification by UC Berkeley, UC Irvine, or UCLA.

9. How to Afford College

I believe that we parents must encourage our children to become educated, so they can get into a good college that we cannot afford.

–Dave Barry,
American author, columnist, and humorist

I am not a financial aid expert. But after guiding college-bound families for several years, I have picked up a few broad-brush ideas. Here are ten considerations for families beginning the college process:

1. Incorporate a financial aid strategy into the college search from day one, instead of at the end. There is nothing more frustrating than your teen landing acceptance at a dream school, only to find your family doesn't qualify for financial aid, or that merit money is not given by that college. Wouldn't it have been better to spend all that time and energy on a school that *does* offer merit scholarships? Up front, compare your initial college list with Kiplinger's "best value" rankings[1] and merit scholarship availability via MeritAid.com.[2] Then refine your college list with affordability in mind.

2. Have a clear strategy and time line for merit scholarships. Scholarships at some schools go to students whose academic credentials are higher than the typical incoming freshman. They offer accomplished students an incentive to attend the school, to raise its statistics, and improve its rankings. Colleges are businesses, and there's no such thing as free merit money! If all the schools on your teen's list are realistic and reach choices, don't expect any academic scholarships.

The logic works like this: If an applicant just "squeaks in" and the admissions department feels they're doing that kid a favor by offering acceptance, there's no reason to offer money too. Conversely, if they think that the kid would be doing *them* a favor by attending, they are likely to offer merit money as an incentive. If your family is too proud to support your child's enrollment at a slightly less prestigious school, don't expect academic scholarships.

Beyond exceptional academic performance, merit money is offered for sports prowess, special arts talents, community service, or multicultural enrichment of the student body. These are not just "gifts": *reciprocity is expected.* Sports scholars are supposed to win for their school. Music award recipients are expected to distinguish the university's ensembles. Community service prizes may include a volunteer project requirement. Multicultural scholars may be asked to participate in special programs.

Pay attention to *timing.* Division I athletics is in a class by itself, requiring that families begin contacting coaches junior year or earlier. Arts scholarships may require portfolios, CDs or Web sites in the fall, followed by live auditions for finalists in the winter (e.g., Bucknell, Lehigh, and Skidmore).

Some scholarship programs require advance applications or nomination by the student's high school in the fall. Finalists visit campus for interviews in winter or spring (e.g., Emory, Vanderbilt, U Virginia, and Elon). If you don't fold scholarships into your upfront planning, you will miss big opportunities.

3. Consider going to university in the UK. Tuition, room and board at a private college in the US runs at least $50K a year. For a public school in state, figure low $20s. In the UK, it's in the low

$30s, and it takes only three years to earn a baccalaureate degree. *You do the math.* But that's a whole lot of airline tickets.

Don't get this bright idea senior year. It's a complicated landscape, so start exploring it sophomore year. And certainly, it is only for the more adventurous, independent student. A helpful primer on going to school outside the US is *Study Away: The Unauthorized Guide to College Abroad* by Mariah Balaban and Jennifer Shields.[4]

4. Don't be too proud to consider a public institution. Skyrocketing private school costs and this decade's recession have clinched it: the age of private school snobbery is over.

Must there be a quality trade-off between public and private higher education? As discussed in chapter three, public institutions are well represented in *US News & World Report's*[5] 2011 rankings of the top fifty national universities. Public schools in the top fifty national universities include: UC Berkeley, UCLA, U Virginia, U Michigan, UNC Chapel Hill, William & Mary, Georgia Tech, UC San Diego, UC Davis, UC Santa Barbara, UC Irvine, U Washington, U Texas Austin, U Wisconsin Madison, Penn State, and U Illinois Urbana-Champaign.

5. Go to community college for the first two years. Enrollments are booming.[5] Most state universities have articulation agreements with community colleges. Students can automatically transfer after earning an associate's degree or completing two years of coursework. For an excellent discussion of community college strategy, I recommend the bestselling classic: *The College Solution: A Guide for Everyone Looking for the Right School at the Right Price* by Lynn O'Shaughnessy.[6]

6. Get a 4 or 5 on five AP tests. If your high school student does well on Advanced Placement exams, he or she can place out of course requirements at most colleges. Every institution has its own system. But generally, if your teen gets 4s or 5s on a semester's worth of courses, that means early graduation and a savings of $25K at a private college.

7. Take summer courses at a public institution. If your kid doesn't place out of a whole semester of courses through APs, get requirements out of the way in summer at a state university. This will still be a bargain if your student is attending a private college full time.

8. Apply *very* selectively for external scholarships. Truth be told, you are *more* likely to get substantial merit money from a college where your kid's credentials are higher than other accepted applicants (e.g., "Presidential" scholarships for which one is automatically considered when accepted). Make sure your college list includes a few safes that your kid would consider attending if the money was there.

That said, it is easy to fill out a FastWeb profile.[7] It especially makes sense if your kid automatically qualifies based on ethnic, racial, or cultural status. Look only for scholarships where the applicant needs to do something reasonable, worth the effort for the amount offered. Prizes are generally $1,000–$2,500, but *every bit helps.* Most kids are too burned out by the college process to write scholarship essays. So somebody who writes well and takes initiative may have a shot. Ben Kaplan's book, *How to Go to College Almost for Free*[8], gives good advice on external scholarships.

9. Join U Promise. U Promise, owned by Sallie Mae, makes contributions to members' 529 savings plans when they make everyday purchases at twenty-one thousand grocery and drug stores, fourteen thousand gas stations, eight thousand restaurants, thousands of retail stores and six hundred online shopping sites.[9] I never go out of my way to buy something from a specific vendor. But it's easy and mindless like airline miles. Frankly, most U Promise members do not earn much because they do not use it consistently, but as an online shopper, I generate a few grand every year, and *every bit adds up.*

10. Fill out need-based aid forms even if you don't think you're eligible. Worst case, you'll get a low-interest loan or work-study. Some scholarship programs require that you fill out a FAFSA and CSS Profile. Become financial aid literate by reading Tim Higgins' *Pay for College without Sacrificing Your Retirement: A Guide to Your Financial Future.* [10] Visit the award-winning Web site, FinAid.org[11], for answers to all your financial aid questions.

10. The Race to Nowhere and the Path to Purpose

Those who have a "why" to live, can bear with almost any "how."

–Viktor Frankl,
Austrian psychiatrist and Holocaust survivor

Vicki Abeles' grassroots documentary film, *The Race to Nowhere*[1], has generated reflection and lively discussion about achievement pressure placed on our nation's children and adolescents. As described on its Web site, the film *"points to the silent epidemic in our schools: cheating has become commonplace, students have become disengaged, stress-related illness, depression and burnout are rampant, and young people arrive at college and the workplace unprepared and uninspired."*[2]

A complete antidote to the issues raised in the film would require a total transformation of American education, parenting, and societal values. I do not pretend to be so ambitious. However, let me plant a few seeds that could be directionally positive.

The Race. Most Americans would probably say, if asked, that they desire higher educational standards to better prepare our children to compete globally. However, most government efforts to raise standards are rote-oriented and content-driven, measured by standardized tests, rather than process-oriented (i.e., ability to think critically, communicate clearly, or problem-solve creatively). Ultimately, there is a disconnect between what most Americans would likely consider to be educational improvement and the ways that government attempts to raise the bar.

At the same time, I believe that American culture suffers from anti-intellectualism, a tendency to defend mediocrity as "normal," and eschew academic excellence as "geekism." The same parents who complain that their kids get too much homework that interferes with "family time" ironically do not seem to have a problem with driving all over the state to get their kids to swim meets and soccer club tournaments.

When I hear about teenager burnout, I question whether academic pressure is the primary culprit. I am more inclined to believe it is overly intense "resume building" that incorporates an impossible schedule of extracurricular activities, *on top of* demanding academics (that is, admittedly, often rote-oriented). If I were to dial down the pressure on college-bound teens, I would prefer to dial down activities before academics. Here's why:

I pointed out in chapter two that grades in college prep courses are the single most important factor considered in college admissions decisions, based on the *NACAC State of College Admission 2010 Report*[3]. This factor drew the highest percentage (87 percent) of colleges attributing "considerable importance" to its impact in admission decisions. By contrast, only 9 percent of colleges surveyed attributed "considerable importance" to the impact of extracurricular activities on admissions decisions. So if your kid is overwhelmed, do you dial back academics, or extracurricular activities?

If you are scratching your head, wondering how this dichotomy can be right, perhaps you have been listening to an urban legend, for which college consultants are, alas, partially responsible. The urban legend is that to get into any desirable college, an applicant must have perfect grades and amazing extracurricular accomplishments.

Not true. This advice resonates for applicants to the Ivy League and other elite colleges. Consultants are focusing on these schools when they proclaim that acceptance requires your kid to earn spectacular grades, perfect test scores, be an Olympic athlete, and have discovered a cure for cancer. But there are 2,500 accredited four-year higher educational institutions in the USA.[4] *Selectivity varies considerably. and there is a school for just about everybody.*

The Destination. So it may be that American high school students are racing with too much of a payload on their backs— overwhelming academics and extracurricular activities. They are also chasing too few schools, whose standards are creeping higher and higher as the baby boomlet drives unreasonable demand for the limited supply of Ivy or otherwise elite degrees.

What's worse, there does not seem to be enough of a prize when students reach their destination, even if it *is* the college of their dreams. The *New York Times* recently ran an article, "College Freshmen Stress Levels High, Survey Finds."[5] The author, Tamar Lewin, quoted results of the 2010 UCLA Higher Education Research Institute and Cooperative Institution Research Program Freshman Survey[6] (which has studied a quarter of a million students entering college for the last forty years), highlighting that self-reported emotional health is at a twenty-five-year low for freshmen. The economy was identified as a possible contributor to the malaise, or at least, an exacerbator.

The recessionary employment outlook may be causing more pain for this generation than for young people of past decades. Psychotherapist Madeline Levine, author of *The Price of Privilege: How Parental Pressure and Material Advantage Are Creating a Generation of Disconnected and Unhappy Kids* [7], identifies both materialism and isolation as factors that are intensifying psychological distress for young people.

Dr. Levine also references the UCLA freshman studies. She laments, "When asked about reasons for going to college in the 1960s and early seventies, most students placed the highest value on 'becoming an educated person' or 'developing a philosophy of life'… Beginning in the 1990s a majority of students say that 'making a lot of money' has become the most important reason to go to college, outranking both the reasons above, as well as 'becoming an authority in my field,' or 'helping others in difficulty.'" She points out the irony that this shift in values coincided with dramatic rises in rates of depression and suicide for this group.[8]

Translation: Our affluent society emphasizes materialism. We pressure our kids to land acceptance at a small group of elite colleges, so that they can make a lot of money. But the recession dims their prospects. So they are devastated. And they do not have nobler, more enduring values to keep them going through this difficult time in our economy.

Psychologist William Damon, director of the Stanford University Center on Adolescence and author of *The Path to Purpose: Helping Our Children Find Their Calling in Life*[9], references his own study of adolescents, in which he found that a fourth were "rudderless." Damon calls these young people *disengaged* (25 percent), while describing the other three categories as *dreamers* (25 percent), *dabblers* (31 percent), and *purposeful* (20 percent).[10]

The *Race to Nowhere* issue is driven by complicated and interwoven cultural, sociological, educational and economic forces. I can only recommend directional steps that individual families can take to begin to transform that race into a path to purpose:

1. Emphasize academics. If something has to be thrown overboard to stave off burnout, let it be extracurricular activities rather than academics. Certainly, there are families in which academics could be dialed down as well, to lower stress and protect sanity. But try editing back on extracurriculars first.

2. Consider a broad range of college alternatives. Expand your horizons beyond the Ivy League with books like Loren Pope's classic, *Colleges That Change Lives: 40 Schools That Will Change the Way You Think About Colleges.*[11] There is a good college fit out there for everybody.

3. Reflect on your own values. What is important to you, and what message are you sending to your child? When you make decisions large and small, what kind of philosophy of life are you modeling? Do the ends justify the means? What are the priorities in your race? *Does the journey matter?*

11. Not Just Getting into College: Parenting for Purpose

What people actually need is not a tensionless state but rather the striving and struggling for some goal worthy of them. What they need is not the discharge of tension at any cost, but the call of a potential meaning waiting to be fulfilled by them.

–Viktor Frankl,
Austrian psychiatrist and Holocaust survivor

Remember the midlife crisis movie *City Slickers*[1]? Billy Crystal played a burned out media sales guy. He found no personal satisfaction in his work, and was embarrassed to speak to his daughter's class on Parents Career Day. When asked what he did for a living, Billy shrugged cynically, "I sell air." Those who have seen this wise, funny film know this was the wake-up call for Billy and his two childhood buddies to go west. With the help of a grizzled old trail boss, "Curly," portrayed by Jack Palance, they discovered that life could be a meaningful adventure.

In my consulting work, I probe a young person's interests and long-term goals. I am often struck by an absence of purpose, even from students with remarkable talent. I once thought my role with college-bound teens was mostly about the "HOW." Now I realize it is even more about the "WHY."

In the previous chapter, I referenced William Damon's significant book, *The Path to Purpose: Helping Our Children Find a Calling in Life.* [2] Professor Damon's book is so rich in wisdom that it warrants more in-depth discussion here. It is based on his adolescent study, in which a quarter of respondents appeared to be rudderless. He refers to these young people as "disengaged" (25 percent), while describing the other three groups as "dreamers" (25 percent), "dabblers" (31 percent), and "purposeful"(20 percent).[3] Damon identifies crucial factors for helping young people develop purpose. He views a parent as a "Socratic coach" who finds everyday opportunities to practice these precepts, upon which I will expand below.[4]

Listen closely for the spark, then fan the flames. Damon offers vivid real-life examples, such as Ryan Hreljac, a first grader who founded Ryan's Well Foundation to bring clean drinking water to children in Africa.[5] Rather than steal Damon's thunder, I will relate an example of my own.

At fourteen, my son was crazy for the guitar. Eric not only played in a blues-rock band, but he also designed and built his own electric guitars from kits. His school required community service hours, so he asked, "Could I do something related to guitar?" Eric mentioned how much the instrument meant to him, and mused that perhaps music could change the life of some needy kid somewhere.

I picked up on his idea, scouting the Web for ways to apply it. Teaching disadvantaged kids to play guitar was not an option for a kid under eighteen. Finally, I came across a fledgling nonprofit headquartered in nearby Montclair, New Jersey, that offered guitar lessons to inner-city kids called Little Kids Rock.[6] Its Web site asked for donations of gently used guitars. It occurred to me that Eric could build guitars and donate them; Eric eagerly took up ownership of the concept.

The nonprofit's charismatic founder, Dave Wish, was thrilled with the idea, and it became a reality. Eric built three guitars that he presented to fifth graders at a charter school in Newark, New Jersey. A decade later, Little Kids Rock is serving 66,000 children in 24 cities nationwide. Eric had the privilege and inspirational experience of being a part of that special program in its infancy.

Take advantage of regular opportunities to open a dialogue. Damon mentions the dinner table as an aspiration "hatching ground." I believe the car or van, the dinner table of this generation, also offers a great venue for picking up on a young person's sparks of interest that may slip out on the way to a soccer game or guitar lesson.

Be open-minded and supportive of the sparks of interest expressed. Damon observes that it's easy to help your teen to build on an idea in an interest area you share. But what if your kid's inner voice is beckoning toward an area that is foreign to you?

My niece Caroline, aged fourteen, is crazy for animals. Her parents are not exactly animal lovers, but they willingly support her passion within the boundaries of practicality.

Caroline owns, loves and cares for a black Lab, as well as a menagerie of cats, birds, lizards, and hamsters. Recently, she became the proud owner of a thoroughbred horse to facilitate her advancing equestrian skills. Caroline goes to summer camp at the Dolphin Research Center in the Florida Keys.[7] We don't know where her passion will lead, but it is poised to direct her life and most likely improve the lives of animals in the future.

Convey your own sense of purpose and the meaning you derive from your work. Damon references an article in the *Wall Street Journal*, pointing out that "today's workers more often spend their time talking on the phone or clicking on a computer than making tangible goods that a child can appreciate. The child is left with the impression that the only thing that is valuable about the parent's work is the paycheck he or she brings home."[8]

When my son, Eric, was a preschooler, he knew Mom's job at Nabisco had something to do with Teddy Grahams, his favorite snack. As he got older, I shared more, creating teachable moments. Now a college student, Eric is considering a Washington Semester.[9] I described a similar program I did during graduate school. From that experience, I gleaned that government bureaucrats often impugn business people with avaricious motives, believing that private sector professionals have no regard for the societal impact of their decisions. This unfortunate hyperbolic view, spun by Hollywood, is held by many young people today. If only parents would talk about the meaning of their work with their kids.

I explained to my son that when I got my MBA, I wanted to find out if that corporate stereotype was accurate. I vowed that there would at least be one scrupulous person in the business world– *me*. My decisions would put people to work; my products would be fair-valued and wholesome; my advertising would be truthful; and I would deal with colleagues and employees with integrity. This is an essential perspective for a young person to hear from his parents. Eric grew up knowing that his parents, both business people, tried to live by principles worth emulating. And a person can change the world in any job, private or public sector.

Impart wisdom about the practicalities of life. No, parents should not dismiss "impractical" careers, like the father who tries to force his son to become a doctor instead of an actor in the film, *Dead Poet's Society*.[10] Rather, Damon clarifies that parents can help adolescents figure out how to make their dreams come true by helping them understand what is realistically required to attain their goals.

Introduce children to potential mentors. Damon's study shows that purposeful youth often look to people outside the home for the ideas and inspiration that help them find purpose. I couldn't agree more about the power of mentors. I have always felt that any great role model who crossed our family's path was somehow a gift from the universe, with something to offer our son beyond what my husband and I could give, to be accepted with gratitude.

Encourage an entrepreneurial attitude. Damon advises cultivating the following attitudes: goal-setting with realistic plans to reach goals; a can-do attitude; persistence in the face of obstacles; tolerance for risk; resilience when encountering failure; determination to achieve measurable results; and resourcefulness in attaining those results.

Nurture a positive outlook. We complain that our kids don't listen to us, but they absorb more than we realize. Damon cautions to beware of messages we unwittingly send. For example, when my mother encountered an obstacle, she would habitually exclaim, "Now we're really in the soup!" Her fatalistic lens was itself an obstacle that I needed to overcome to become an achiever.

Instill in children a feeling of agency, linked to responsibility. Damon encourages sending the message that our kids' dreams *matter,* and they *can* make them come true. He urges parents to teach their adolescents the realistic requirements of achieving goals, and create expectations that their kids will take on responsibility. My niece Caroline grooms and tacks her horse, participates in agility training with her black Lab, and cleans her critters' cages (with a bit of help from Dad).

Ironically, the ancient Greeks used the term *daimon* to describe an individual's guiding force that calls that person to his or her unique destiny.[11] *William Damon* encourages parents to do all they can to help their children hear and respond to that special call.

III. The First Two Years of High School

12. First Day of High School

Uh...It's My First Day!

−Homer Simpson,
Cartoon character created by Matt Groening

Your teenager is psyched with anticipation, worried by insecurity. You've cleaned out Staples and Aerospatiale. *OMG!* Sometime this week, your baby will begin ninth grade, the first year of high school.

In some cases, the transition is a bigger deal than in others. If your teen is going from a local middle school to a regional high school, it means a larger, more anonymous environment requiring more independence. If your student is transferring from a public to a private school setting, it will mean an entirely new set of classmates, a ramping up of academic rigor, and humbling grade deflation.

It is the start of a new chapter of adolescent development. You have survived middle school, so you feel you can take on *any* challenge! You're probably right. (From middle school, after all, there's nowhere to go but up.) Each developmental stage is unique. You'll be encountering dating, driving, drinking, drugs, defiance, and depression: all the dreaded "D" words. And it will end with your child's "D-parting" for college.

Guidebooks to the roller-coaster ride that began when your child turned thirteen include: *The Primal Teen: What the New Discoveries about the Teenage Brain Tell Us about Our Kids* by Barbara

Strauch [1] and *Get Out of My Life, But First Could You Drive Me to the Mall? A Parent's Guide to the New Teenager, Revised and Updated,* by Anthony E. Wolf. [2]

Here are three tips on what you can do now to help *naturally* begin to position your ninth grader for college without stress or overkill.

1. Take a four-year planning approach to course selection. Meet with the guidance counselor early this fall for perspective. Of course, your ninth grader is already enrolled, but an early counselor meeting can determine if any modifications need to be made.

The minimum "college prep" curriculum for most U.S. colleges includes: four years of English, including literature and composition; three years of math, including algebra I & II and geometry; three of laboratory science, including biology and chemistry; three years of social studies/science, including geography, US history, world cultures; and two years of the same world language.

College Board[3] advises a fourth year of mathematics (trigonometry, calculus, or statistics); says many colleges require more than two years of foreign language; suggests arts electives to exercise the mind in unique ways; and a computer course.

It is advisable to maximize academic options from the outset, ensuring your teen can qualify for AP courses junior or senior year. Some high schools require an honors class as a prerequisite for AP, with a grade cutoff. Some schools even require an entry test, because they don't have enough AP sections to accommodate everyone.

This is why it is a good idea to meet with the guidance counselor early on to understand your school's requirements. Does your teen need to be in all honors or AP courses? No, the goal is not to overwhelm your kid, Every student has to find the best balance for his or her skill set and interests. In my view, it is better to get mostly As in a combination of AP, honors, and standard college prep courses than all Bs in all APs. Advise your teen to pick subjects in which he or she excels, and go for advanced versions of only those courses.

Try not to be talked into a "no honors" approach by an overly conservative counselor or an under confident student. This will lock the student out of advanced classes from the outset and limit flexibility later. In my practice, I sometimes see capable students performing poorly in regular college prep courses because *they are bored* with the pace and are not sufficiently challenged by their peers. In retrospect, their parents speculate that they may have done better in more advanced classes. As discussed in chapter two, the two most important factors for college admission are grades in "solids" and curriculum rigor.[4] Keep that delicate balance in mind throughout your teen's high school years.

2. Communicate priorities. Clarify for your freshman that *school comes first,* which will make decision-making simpler and less painful throughout high school. Otherwise, your student can easily become overwhelmed and confused by the pressures of academic ramp-up versus middle school, the vast array of extra-curricular activity options, and the physiological, emotional and social challenges every teenager faces. A clear message of priorities from the outset will prevent *Race to Nowhere* [5] burnout. If something has to be sacrificed for the sake of mental health, your teenager knows from the outset that it will not be academics.

Prioritizing academics may feel like forcing a kid to eat Brussels sprouts. But it may simply be our anti-intellectual culture that discounts the stimulation, satisfaction and inspiration that comes from learning a fascinating subject or solving a challenging problem. Academics can be a delight when a love of learning is cultivated within a family from the very beginning. And generally, it will be academic abilities that will determine your child's future.

3. Begin financial preparation for college. *It's never too early for this, especially in a recessionary economy.* Become a regular reader of Kiplinger's Web site[6] and Lynn O'Shaughnessy's College Solution blog.[7] Ask your guidance counselor about community workshops for parents on financial aid. Talk to your accountant or financial adviser about investing for college.

13. Ten Things Parents Can Do for Your College-Bound Tenth Grader

Adolescence is a period of rapid changes. Between the ages of twelve and seventeen, for example, a parent ages as much as twenty years.

—Anonymous

When our son was a sophomore, we kept wondering what, if anything, we should be doing to prepare for college. We did not want to freak him out by launching the college process too soon. But as conscientious parents, we did not want to be asleep at the wheel, either. We did not hit the right balance immediately, but we finally settled into a reasonable rhythm. Here are ten guidelines for tenth grade, facilitating valuable high school experience while subtly laying the groundwork for college.

1. Prevent transcript disasters. Your student doesn't have to nail a perfect GPA to get into most colleges on the planet, but avoid red flags wherever possible. Get your son or daughter extra help (from the teacher, student tutors, or paid tutors) earlier rather than later, with no apologies. If your student gets a C for a marking period, it is not a catastrophe, but it *is* a wake-up call. Then it is up to *you* to initiate damage control, to ensure that the average is brought up to avoid a C on the final transcript.

Continue to send the message that your family places *academics* first on the priority list. If anything seems to interfere with your student's grades, such as extracurricular activities, nonessential employment, social life or social media, clarify that these other pursuits must be balanced appropriately with academics. If you suspect more serious issues, learning or emotional, contact an educational consultant or mental health professional to help your child.

2. Scout for summer programs that help your student explore interests. As a starting point for Internet research on the best summer exploratory programs, pick up *Ultimate Guide to Summer Opportunities for Teens: 200 Programs that Prepare You for College Success* by Sandra Berger.[1] Scouting for summer programs is one of many ways a parent can follow William Damon's advice to "fan the flame"[2] of a young person's spark of interest. It is not just about becoming your student's summer concierge; it is about being a resourceful agent responding to your teen's germinating interests. Your teen may not quite know where to go with a budding interest, and you can help find a venue for exploring it.

3. Encourage your teen to seek challenge in academic areas of strength. As mentioned earlier, a student need not take all AP or honors courses. The number of advanced courses on a high school transcript is completely individual, influenced by a student's unique skill set, school size and setting, and the specific programs offered by the school. However, encourage your son or daughter to *try* advanced courses in subjects in which he or she feels confident. *Even if it is only one.*

Seeking challenge is not just about the transcript. It is about your student delving deeper into a subject in which he or she is especially gifted, actualizing one's potential and perhaps finding one's calling. Your son or daughter's intellectual development is exploding at age fifteen, just like every other dimension of his or her life. In an advanced class, your student can plunge into a favorite subject's fascinating higher mysteries, with peers who are operating on the same level. The teacher will not be weighed down by instructing students who are struggling with fundamentals or completely indifferent; the teacher will have more time to focus on your student's more advanced questions. Mentorship is more likely to develop in an advanced class.

4. Help your teen seek depth versus breadth in extracurricular activities. There are three reasons for pursuing extracurricular activities: to explore interests, develop commitment, and enjoy life through expression of one's talents and passions. It's all about self-discovery, *not* getting into college. No kidding, academic credentials are the chief ingredient for college acceptance. Beyond strong academics, colleges are interested in a student who is a jack of a few trades and a master of one or two. The *Race to Nowhere* [3] mentality is entrenched in our "soccer mom" culture, but it is not really coming from the colleges.

Encourage your student to "go deep" in a few areas he or she *truly enjoys,* seeking leadership positions, awards, and higher skill levels. *Don't* let your teen get spread thin by superficial involvement in too many pursuits. Teach your son or daughter to prioritize and edit back superfluous activities, leading by example. "Editing back" is a life lesson many of us parents could benefit from learning ourselves.

5. Provide clerical support. Make a *file box*. Start collecting things that your kid would otherwise *lose*: test results, transcripts, awards, sports results, community service hours, and great essays. Don't go crazy, don't insist on your teen's involvement, just quietly *do it,* so everything will be organized in one place next year when you need it. Chefs call this approach *"mise en place"* (everything in place). Get the ingredients ready so you've got them right there when you need them.

6. If you do visit a campus, make it part of a fun family trip and low-key it. It is *anxiety producing* for your sophomore to seriously consider the idea that high school will end and he or she will be moving away from home. Teens live in *"the NOW"*; therefore, college is a remote, surrealistic concept for sophomores. If a desirable college is a convenient stop on a family trip, walk the campus, but you don't need to enroll in an information session just yet. A low-key campus walk can help a students file away *mental pictures* of what an acceptable college might look and feel like. That's all you want right now.

If other families are visiting campuses this early, you may feel like you are remiss by not doing so. We are all affected by our peers, parents as well as children. Misguided parents who are prematurely stressing about the college process are doing harm, not only to their own teenagers, but to the whole school community by escalating the "hype." Try to follow your own inner compass. Restraint will serve your adolescent best.

7. Foster a positive relationship with your child, and choose parent-teen battles carefully. White water rapids are up ahead, and you need all the goodwill possible to preserve a loving, constructive, honest relationship with your adolescent. You eventually will experience the *"perfect storm"* when your adolescent's normal, powerful drive for autonomy eventually collides with the college application process. Don't create it too early. Protect goodwill: you will need it.

8. If you want to do "advanced recon" research on colleges that fit your child's interests, make it stealth research only. With some exceptions, it's too early for most teens to care. They have other things to worry about that are more pertinent to being sophomores. If your teen has well-developed interests in specific areas that warrant researching specialty college programs, that might be a reason to do some investigative reading or seeking out families with older kids who may be able to offer a blueprint with perspective. Do it quietly, keep it to yourself, and file it away for later.

9. Encourage your teen to build relationships with teachers, employers, coaches, and counselors. Colleges prefer recommendations from eleventh grade teachers, but kids don't automatically know how to build relationships with adults. *Now is when your teen can learn not to hide in the back.* Urge your son or daughter to participate in class, ask thoughtful questions, advocate respectfully when there is a problem, deliver on responsibilities, and gain the confidence of adult supervisors. This approach may lead to more than just a college recommendation; it could result in the formation of a mentoring relationship lasting for many years to come. And being assertive with adults is a life skill that will help your student in college and beyond.

10. Support your adolescent's growth and development as a complete human being. Your son or daughter needs support for physical and mental health, getting enough sleep, eating right, and managing stress. Who is going to help with all that if not Mom or Dad? The world would be happy to "use up" your adolescent (e.g., demanding teachers, athletic coaches, theater directors, and later employers). Right now, only you stand between the world and your adolescent, modeling boundary-setting and encouraging self-care. The boundaries you establish now will be internalized as your teenager grows to adulthood.

Your young person's life needs to be enriched in higher-level dimensions: spiritual, ethical, intellectual, aesthetic, social, and emotional. You can help by being a caring, involved adult guide who is not too invasive but "always there" as a sounding board. Raising a well-developed human being is ultimately the best way to position your student for college.

14. High School Testing Strategy and Timeline

The best way out is always through.

–Robert Frost,
American poet

The alarm clock rings, startling me out of REM sleep. I grab it furiously, switch it off, and hurl it to the floor. Then I glance at the time, and—*YIKES! I'm late!* I leap out of bed. It's Saturday morning and I'm *missing the SATs!* I'm in a cold sweat until I realize it's just a dream. *Whew!* I'm fifty-five, my son is in college, and...I don't ever have to take the SATs again. But I still have that nightmare. *Doesn't everybody?*

Every day, I advise students still living that nightmare. Recalling my own test anxiety, I recommend a schedule of standardized tests that gets the biggest bang for the least amount of testing. Still, I suggest whatever regimen that is practical for a student's specific goals. Let's go through a potential test schedule, year by year, and I'll show you what is optional and what is not.

Ninth grade: No worries yet. If your student has a passion for life sciences or a pre-health career and is enrolled in freshman biology, encourage him or her to take the SAT II Biology Subject Test It is a good idea to take it in June after mastering the year's content and it is still fresh in his or her mind.

A word about SAT II Subject Tests: a student should take them only if he or she is proficient in the subject. Your student does not take these tests with a general college-bound population; he or she will take them with kids who excel in this subject. For example, if your student scores 700 in biology, he or she is only in the 84th percentile in that highly skewed group. In contrast, 700 in the SAT I Math section will place the student in the 93rd percentile of the broader population taking that test.[1]

Tenth grade: In most high schools, your student will take the PSAT (Preliminary SAT I) twice (in school, in October). It is truly practice for sophomores, in school under genuine test conditions. Should you encourage your sophomore to practice with a test book? I say *yes:* success breeds confidence. However, it is too early to stress your teen out about testing. He or she has not had all the math necessary to ace it, so interpret results with a grain of salt.

The ninth grade biology approach works for tenth grade too. If your student is interested in pre-health, especially accelerated medicine, he or she should take SAT II Chemistry in June after a year of chemistry. A verbally geared student can take SAT II Literature if familiar with British and American literature, but the student should review a test book for terminology on figurative language.

Tenth grade testing decisions should be case-by-case and opportunistic. My son's high school offered the full AP US History curriculum in tenth grade, so he took SAT II US History in May, immediately after the AP Test. Encourage your student to register for an SAT II Subject Test after a year of content, while it is still *fresh in his or her mind!*

If you suspect that your student has learning or attention issues, whether or not he or she is classified in school, tenth grade would be a good time to get a diagnosis from an independent learning consultant. The learning consultant provides the documentation needed to apply for extra time accommodation on standardized tests. Assume it will take at least six months to get approval from testing organizations.

Eleventh grade: *The year from standardized testing hell.* First, your junior will take the PSAT-NMSQT in school in October. This one counts, not with the colleges, but for the National Merit Scholarship Program.[2]

Of the 1.5 million NMSP entrants, about fifty thousand qualify for recognition. More than two-thirds of qualifiers receive Letters of Commendation; a third of the fifty thousand become semifinalists, 94 percent of whom go on to become finalists. Over half the finalists are selected for merit scholarships. When applying to college, your kid will be thrilled to have a few academic awards to fill in. NMS Commendation is a great one. Qualifying scores vary by state. (Alas, my state, New Jersey, has the highest cutoff score.)

Now, the burning question: Should your kid take the SAT, ACT, or both? Your junior has essentially taken the SAT I *twice*, since the PSAT is so similar. You get junior year PSAT results by December. If disappointed, register for ACT in February, with tutoring if you can afford it.

By the end of February, you will know which test to choose. Compare SAT versus ACT scores by looking at Internet comparison charts. Your student will then either sign up to take the ACT again to slightly improve, or abandon the ACT and go SAT all the way. Once it is clear which test favors your student's skill set, do not continue to take both: that would truly be unnecessary testing overkill. All US colleges accept both tests, and they are viewed as equally "valid." The SAT/ACT test date pattern goes like this: Jan-SAT, Feb-ACT, Mar-SAT (no subject tests), Apr-ACT, May-SAT, Jun-both, Sep-both, Oct-both, Nov-SAT, Dec-both.

Next burning question: *How many times should your teen take the SAT or ACT, once he or she has decided on one or the other?* It varies by individual, but I say *twice is nice, no more than thrice.* Both the SAT and ACT offer a choice of which *test dates* to send in. (However, when colleges look at SAT scores from multiple test dates, they take the highest score from each section.)

June of junior year, take an SAT II Subject Test in Math. Math Level 1 tests algebra, geometry, basic trigonometry, algebraic functions, and elementary statistics. Math Level 2 covers numbers and operations; algebra and functions; coordinate, three-dimensional and trigonometric geometry; data analysis, statistics and probability.

Compass Educational Group[3] suggests that a student needs to have completed precalculus with a solid B or better to feel comfortable on Math 2. The content of the Math 1 test extends only through Algebra II and basic trigonometry. Only quantitative college majors, such as engineering, require Math 2.

Twelfth grade: Your teen will probably retake SAT I or ACT during senior year fall, as well as a few SAT II Subject tests, depending on how selective his or her college list is. Compass[4] offers a list of *what is required where*. Some schools "require" SAT IIs, some "recommend" them, some only "consider" them. Specialized majors and accelerated programs may demand more than their university requires. Some schools do not require SAT II tests if you take the ACT with Writing, so check each school's Web site for specifics.

Delay foreign language tests until November, assuming your senior is still studying the language. The test-taker should be as advanced in the language as possible. November offers "with listening," which sounds difficult, but actually is not.

"STOP!" you say. "You said you were going to help us *minimize testing!"* Depending on where your student applies, he or she may actually need NO standardized tests. There is a wide spectrum of variation in requirements, which requires up-front clarification of the testing required by the schools on the college list. As the college list is developed, create a spreadsheet indicating the testing required for each school.

The most elite national universities, such as the Ivies, generally require the most standardized tests. If your student is applying to a public university, he will need the SAT I or ACT, because state schools place more emphasis on quantitative credentials. However, public institutions do not require SAT II Subject Tests.

Some colleges that require SAT IIs will waive that requirement if an applicant takes ACT with Writing. Many small private liberal arts colleges are now test optional, listed at FairTest.org.[5] So you may not have to wake up from that recurring dream for the rest of your life.

15. First Aid for a Disappointing Grade

Failure is not an option.

–Gene Kranz,
Mission Control of Apollo 13

Sometime during high school, your adolescent will earn a disappointing grade. "Disappointing" is a relative term, based on your family's expectations. So interpret it within the context of your situation. Here are some considerations, depending on the timing and duration of the problem:

1. Marking period. Ask why. Is it *skill, pace, effort, time,* or *teacher?* If it's a *skill* problem, create a dialogue with the teacher. Get extra help. Nip it in the bud now. If it's *pace,* your high school student may be in a class too advanced for his or her aptitude in the subject. Early on, your teen could drop back, gaining consolidation time to absorb concepts and perform better. Although it is advisable for a high school student to take AP or honors courses in areas of strong aptitude, too many advanced classes or inappropriate placement can upset the balance between challenge and grade performance, as well as burning out and discouraging the student.

An *effort* problem may be due to lack of interest in the subject, a distracting classroom situation, or a social-emotional issue. Hopefully, you have the positive dynamics with your teen to discuss what may be going on. It is also helpful to reflect on the value your family places on academics, and whether you are clearly communicating to your child that school performance *matters* in your household.

Your student may not have *time* to keep up with course demands. Sit down with your student and look at the course load and extracurricular activities. This grade may be a wake-up call that your kid is doing too much, and needs help prioritizing, editing back, or managing time.

Let's face it, we've all had a *teacher* who didn't explain concepts or assess skills well, lacked a rubric, had a personality that clashed with students, or was downright unfair. Life lessons can be learned here: should the student switch or stick it out, self-advocate or involve parents? It calls for a parent's wisdom, discernment, and finesse, leading by example.

2. Annual grade. Hopefully, a disappointing marking period will result in intervention that will improve the situation, or at least damage control, before it translates into a final transcript grade. However, turnaround may not be possible within the year.

Perhaps *skill* problems were not caught early enough or extra help was insufficient. Maybe it was too late to switch to a slower *pace* class. *Effort* may not have improved. Your student may not have found *time* for success in this subject, due to extracurricular commitments, like sports obligations until the season was over. Or a *teacher* situation may have been unsolvable.

When an academic problem translates into an annual grade, it may be a broader issue. It may be the kid's *aptitude* in the subject. It is possible that a science student may succeed in biology, which is largely content, but not "get" chemistry or physics, which both involve mathematical thinking. A student may reach an aptitude ceiling, perceived or real, in subjects requiring logical-mathematical, spatial, or linguistic intelligence.

There could be a major *balance* dilemma between extracurricular activities and academics. Priorities need to be reassessed going forward. Perhaps your teen does athletics every season. He or she may need to cut back a sport or take a lighter load next year. These are tough family decisions, which often are ultimately resolved by a family's values.

As I have emphasized throughout this book, colleges are *academic institutions*. Extracurricular accomplishments are not sufficient compensation for problem grades. If mediocre grades are deemed acceptable within the family as a trade-off for extracurricular involvement, it is a matter of fact that prospects at selective colleges will be diminished.

Sometimes there are *extenuating circumstances* driving a problem with grades, such as an undiagnosed LD, illness, relocation, divorce, loss, or a mental health issue. Grades can be a red flag signaling need for a learning evaluation, psychotherapeutic counseling, or medical support. Although individuals differ, girls are more likely to open up about emotional issues; boys may silently soldier on, simply leaving behavioral clues such as letting grades slip. Depending on how your adolescent deals with problems, you may need to do some real detective work to ferret out what is wrong.

If grades are the outward signal of an inward issues, be thankful for this benign wake-up call, rather than more destructive, irreversible behavior. It is advantageous to be able to diagnose and address an adolescent's issues now, while still living at home. Once your son or daughter moves on to college, there will be far less close and caring supervision of learning, emotional and health issues.

3. What year? If a grade problem occurs in ninth or tenth grade, *address it quickly* and move on. From a college standpoint, an early grade problem is not a disaster, since admissions departments always consider *"trend."* Your adolescent is a growing work-in-progress, and admissions people "get" this. If there is a precipitous grade drop in junior year, however, it signals a *"downward trend,"* which they don't like to see.

If it's a junior year problem, you need to address it more decisively: there is *no luxury of time.* Take a hard look at your teen's senior year fall, both academic schedule and extracurricular activities. Encourage your student to swing into action. Course load must be balanced between challenging and realistic courses, to re-establish an academic *"upward trend."* Eliminate nonessential activities: the *"utility"* of an improved GPA beats one more club membership. If senior year fall flexibility is minimal, get a jump on the admissions process during the summer. Encourage your student to begin filling out applications and write essays before school begins.

16. Ten Ways for Teens to Spend the Summer

Summer afternoon – Summer afternoon...the two most beautiful words in the English language.

–William James,
Nineteenth C. American psychologist and philosopher

Parents often ask me how high school students can best spend the summer. Here are ten alternatives:

1. "Do nothing." This approach goes back to educator Thomas Mann, who fought the forty-eight-week school year in the 1840s, because he believed that "over-stimulating young minds could lead to instability or insanity."[1]

Should parents discourage kids from doing *anything* in summer? Are they so fragile they will break under pressure? We've all heard parents decrying the demands of today's culture: "*Our parents just threw open the back screen door, told us to go out and play, and we never came home until supper.*"

Nostalgic: but helpful? Like most boomers, I fondly recall running barefoot in fragrant, freshly mowed grass on summer evenings, catching fireflies, and listening for the Mister Softie truck. *Great memory!* But it doesn't need to be every summer, all summer. After a few weeks of down time, I believe most young people are ready for some structure and stimulation.

2. Exploration of alternatives. How about trying something new? Self-discovery is a teen's *number one* developmental task.

Summer programs (academic, wilderness, arts, sports, travel, service) give adolescents a chance to experiment in an untapped interest or talent area, meeting kids who enjoy similar pursuits.

I have mentioned the excellent *Ultimate Guide to Summer Opportunities for Teens: 200 Programs that Prepare You for College Success* by Sandra Berger.[2] Another good resource is *The Complete Guide to the Gap Year: The Best Things to Do between High School and College* by Kristin White,[3] since many gap program organizations also do summer versions of their gap programs.

One fine exploration program is Lead America.[4] It teaches a leadership process within a career content area, such as Engineering & Robotics, Medicine & Healthcare, Business & Entrepreneurship, Law & Trial, Law & Justice, Government & Politics, Security & Intelligence, Digital Media & Journalism, and Theatre Arts. Programs are held throughout the country on elite college campuses.

Is it *necessary* for a college applicant to have such experiences? *Absolutely not!* Colleges know many students cannot afford exotic summer programs. They do not want applications to be transparent measures of a family's wealth. However, if you can swing it, programs *can* be a true gift of self-discovery for your child.

3. Remedial academic catch-up. It can be tutoring, a local class, or online course. Depending on your teen's situation, it may be crucial to circumvent an academic slide, or vital for managing learning disabilities.

4. Advance preparation for next year. *Not just for geeks!* Get ahead if fall holds tough courses or standardized tests. This can be a local preview class, online courses, books, or tutoring.

5. Enrichment and creative renewal. This can be an arts workshop, wilderness camp, leadership program, travel experience, local gifted student class, or an inspired summer reading list.

Examples of superb teen programs include: Broadreach,[5] Overland,[6] and Where There Be Dragons.[7]

6. Family and friendship time. Traveling or at home, the shore, or the lake, summer is great for solidifying family (and extended family) relationships. This window is only open for a short time—and it closes so quickly. Summer also offers more time to build or renew friendships, especially if during the school year a teen's pursuits are more of a solo nature.

7. Extracurricular mastery. If a student has a passionate interest, it is often a year-round one. Most parents know that a serious athlete needs involvement in that sport all year to be competitive, so training camps, sports clubs, and regional or national competitions are a fact of life for those kids. Performers advance skills via summer intensives and performance experiences, and visual artists create portfolios.

However, parents can help a young person strike a *balance* between becoming a "technician" and *developing as a human being.* Parents can support a teen's aspirations while adding a gentle reality check, keeping their own egos and dreams in perspective. Parents can help create boundaries that will protect a teen's self-esteem and prevent burnout.

8. Earning money. I am often asked if paid employment is as acceptable to admissions committees as summer enrichment programs. The answer is *yes.* A job will help your adolescent develop responsibility and character that will not only impress colleges, it will build a lifelong worth ethic. Your family's needs and child's preferences should dictate. Hours worked will demonstrate the student's motivation and time management skills on the application.

For teenagers so inclined, summer can also be a time for trying an entrepreneurial venture, somewhere between a lemonade stand and the founding of Facebook. I have had high school clients who managed rock bands, started gardening services, and created their own Web sites.

9. Giving back. Kids who serve give and receive *intrinsic benefits*. Opportunities to help others and solve problems abound, through church, school, scouts, hospitals, local volunteer squads, animal rescue organizations, community agencies, disease foundations, parks, or programs like Habitat for Humanity.[8]

National organizations measure extensive commitment and recognize it with prestigious awards, which may help a service-oriented student dimensionalize his or her efforts for admissions or scholarship committees. Examples include: participation in the Congressional Award for Youth program; [9] membership in an organization that recognizes character, such as the National Honor Society; [10] or a senior scout rank accomplishment, such as Boy Scouts of America Eagle Scout [11] or Girl Scouts of America Gold Award. [12]

My own feeling is that public service, as expressed in a student's essays, be "from the heart"—*not* just something to round out the resume. Yes, colleges are impressed, and a student's hard work in this area certainly deserves recognition. But winning admissions brownie points is a jaded motivation for community service, part of the *Race to Nowhere* [13] mentality. Sadly, it is often parents themselves who encourage this cynical kind of thinking. Service has its own intrinsic rewards; parents can help their teenagers appreciate the satisfaction that service can bring through sharing their own perspectives and modeling a service orientation themselves. Moreover, teenage service activities may provide the foundation for a young person's discovery of his or her life purpose.

10. Responsibility and leadership. These key qualities can be developed in summer camps, sports and arts activities, family responsibilities, paid employment, and community service. So—do anything over the summer, *anything but nothing!*

IV. Junior Year of High School

17. Your Eleventh Grader's Eleven Steps to Success

Courage doesn't always roar. Sometimes courage is the quiet voice at the end of the day saying, "I will try again tomorrow."

—Mary Anne Radmacher,
American writer and artist

Junior year is here: The year that counts. Maybe your teen made mistakes, didn't focus enough, experienced a few "blip" grades last year. But now...*it's time to get serious!*

What does that mean, exactly? *Be perfect?* Get an electrode zap from genius headgear like in science fiction comedies? Never allow your teen to have *any* fun until the "fat envelope" comes from the dream college a year and a half from now? *Of course not.* As discussed in chapter ten, the last thing you want is your high school student to stress so much that he or she arrives at the dream school completely burned out, bringing no joy or inspiration to college. Here are eleven general guidelines:

1. Dial down extracurriculars. Does your teen do two varsity sports? Reduce it to one. Did your teen spend every night out last year on stage crew for the musical, even though he or she doesn't plan a theater career? Skip it this year. Unless that pizza delivery job is critical to family finances, persuade your teen to work only in the summer. One more club, one more karate belt, won't make a difference in college admission opportunities. As I have emphasized throughout this book, do not sacrifice academics, or your teen's sanity, on the altar of extracurricular activities.

Yes, it's hard to edit back, especially when you're so proud of your kid's dazzling accomplishments. But don't be tempted to say, "Let's see how it goes." Often the wake-up call that a teenager is doing too much is a grade disaster during junior year. Time and again I have seen this scenario replay with families in my consulting practice. *You do not want that wake-up call:* it may be too late to recover, and colleges want to see an upward trend. It's your job, as a parent, to preempt pitfalls by being one step ahead, and editing back activities before they become overwhelming.

2. Help your teen find a good balance between academic challenge and overkill. It is advisable for an eleventh grader to challenge him or herself in areas of strength, so suggest taking honors courses and an AP if available in the student's favorite subjects. Colleges want to see that an applicant has sought challenge consistent with his or her skill set, and it is advisable for you to create such expectations in your family.

If your student has already "missed the window" for advanced courses in junior year, urge him or her to knock it out of the park this year to be considered for some advanced courses senior year. Colleges want to see not only an upward trend in grades, but also an elevation in self-challenge. Admissions officers do not like to see a student slacking off senior year.

Once again, however, I do not recommend saddling your student with more honors or APs than he or she can handle, whether it be junior or senior year. Yes, advanced courses are worth more in high school and college weighting systems than regular courses, but *don't sacrifice grade performance.* This is especially true in rigorous private schools, where grade deflation can sometimes under represent a student's aptitude and effort, especially compared to a uniformly talented, intense student population.

Academics get tricky junior year, since many subjects ramp up significantly in terms of conceptual difficulty. Eleventh grade is also the first time most students will take Advanced Placement courses. AP's typically cover a tremendous amount of content, and much of it is unfortunately rote material. Further, performing well in an AP class is not a guarantee of acing the College Board AP test in May. It is the student's responsibility to put in the intensive hours of study required to master the test material, through review books in addition to the high school textbooks.

At the same time, junior year can also be a academically pivotal year for some students. You will notice when your student is beginning to hit his or her stride. It is an individual thing, but eleventh grade is when many young people start gaining traction on independent study habits; begin to integrate conceptual learning from related subjects; develop the intellectual maturity to appreciate philosophically complex issues; and begin to feel burgeoning enthusiasm for a specific field of study.

3. Spring for a tutor. Whether it is for SAT or ACT tests or a course with which your student is struggling, I say *go for it*. If you can afford it, "tutor often and early" before an academic problem becomes insurmountable.

Tutoring is a better financial investment than paying for extra-curricular lessons, unless your student is headed for Division I sports or a music conservatory. Getting a tutor also sends a message to your teen that academic performance is valued in your family and you are willing to pay for extra help if your student takes the tutoring seriously and practices between sessions.

Tutoring is not a "badge of shame" that your child is an underachiever or unmotivated. One-on-one tutoring is a time-honored, powerfully effective way to learn; it's just not as cost-efficient as classroom teaching. The pedagogical approach at Oxford and Cambridge is entirely tutor-based. Can you imagine taking piano lessons in a class of thirty kids? When hands-on learning, mentoring motivation, or diagnosis of systematic errors is required, tutoring is often the best key to unlock the door.

4. Prepare for the PSATs. You may hear no, it's just for practice. Such advice is inherently silly. Would your student athlete not practice skills before a game, just because it is not the final championship? Would your student musician not warm up before a choral concert?

National Merit Scholarship[1] qualifications are based on PSAT performance. Whether or not your student needs money, it is advisable to achieve a commendation level. Good PSAT performance also sets in motion an upward spiral of confidence that will be needed with all the testing your child will take over the coming year.

5. Set aside this year's spring break for college visits. Your guidance counselor will present junior college night in January and work with your student on developing a college list during the winter. If this is not happening, you may want to enlist the help of an independent consultant. But edit back business trips and family plans so that when your eleventh grader is on break you can visit campuses.

6. Educate yourself. Don't drive your teen crazy too early. Simply reinforce the value of academics, and encourage your teen to work hard and get good grades. Meanwhile, quietly build up your knowledge through reading college admissions books. Talk with parents who have experienced the college process, but only those who will give you sound advice without stressful hype.

7. Prepare financially. Hopefully, you have been talking to your accountant or financial adviser, and taking his or her advice about investing for college. Now it is time to become even more focused on the specifics of financial aid and merit scholarships, through community workshops, books and Web sites mentioned in chapter nine. It is wise to build your family's financial considerations into the college search now, rather than when you're halfway through the process.

8. Preserve a constructive, honest dialogue with your adolescent. Junior year is tough. This is the year of the junior prom and all that goes with it, perhaps the first big dating relationship or breakup, learners permit or drivers license, and the ever-present danger of teenage rebellion and risky behaviors. Add to all of these rites of passage the inherently explosive college search and application process. As a parent, you will have to be both a tough boundary-setter and a wise, empathetic counselor. Somehow, you will need to find a way to protect goodwill and a healthy dynamic that will help your adolescent make positive choices in all areas, including the college process.

9. Channel your micromanaging tendencies into clerical support. Keep building the *file box* discussed in chapter thirteen. You can now expand the file to include information on specific colleges as your family visits campuses. My sister fondly called her daughter's file the "Box o' Colleges." Your high school student most likely will not hold onto these resources, but will be pleased and relieved that you have them at your fingertips when needed.

10. Encourage your teen to build relationships with eleventh grade teachers. Colleges prefer recommendations from junior year teachers. It is essential for your teen to become assertive about participating in class, become a visible leader, and actively develop relationships with these teachers. This will not only to make it easier to ask for a recommendation at the end of junior year, but because confident self-advocacy and forming mentoring relationships are also valuable life skills that will serve your son or daughter well from now on.

11. Support your teen's growth and development as a complete human being. This has been true all through high school, and may even be more crucial during the stressful junior year. Underneath all the academic, extracurricular, and social pressure, as well as the looming college process, your adolescent is navigating a profound journey, wrestling with big questions of identity and purpose. In my view, a parent's stewardship of a growing young adult must offer guidance and empathy for that journey. Everything else follows.

18. Calendar for High School Juniors

Never before have we had so little time in which to do so much.

–Franklin D. Roosevelt,
Thirty-second President of the United States

Ellen DeGeneres recently shared "Ellen's Funniest Calendars"[1] on her TV talk show, inspiring me to publish my own Position U 4 College calendar for families with high school juniors starting the college process. My calendar isn't as fun as some Ellen found, such as "Nuns Having Fun." Then again, I am not quite as funny as Ellen. I do, however, try to take stress out of the college process. Here is my concise **Calendar for High School Juniors:**

January: Meet with your guidance counselor, an SAT or ACT tutor, and a college consultant. Formulate ideas of what you are looking for in a college (size, location, setting, programs, academic atmosphere, extracurricular activities, social climate, weather). Decide how to go with testing based on PSAT results.

February: Work on your college list, researching colleges online and visiting on winter break. Plan your summer program.

March: Begin standardized testing, following either the SAT (March) or ACT (April) timeline. Keep those grades up! Visit a college or two during spring break.

April: Study for AP tests with prep books. If your AP subject dovetails with an SAT II subject (e.g., AP US or European History), schedule it in May during APs. *Learn the content only once!*

May: Ask teachers for recommendations. Offer your teachers ammunition: questionnaires that some high schools request, a resume to show a full picture of your achievements, and a paper you wrote for that teacher. End of junior year may seem early, but beating the fall rush is considerate of a teacher's time.

June: Swing for the bleachers with eleventh grade cumulative testing and standardized tests. Visit a college that offers summer courses so there will be students on campus to observe. Start journaling as a way of preparing to write college essays.

July: Enjoy your summer program, travel with your family, or your life guarding job. If you want to prepare for college, keep a journal to get in the mind-set for writing essays. Otherwise, just refresh and renew.

August: Party's over. When the Common Application goes online, you can fill out the clerical part. You can start brainstorming essay ideas. The last week of August, when colleges are in full swing, visit before you start school yourself.

September: Time to recalibrate your college list based on what you've learned over the summer. Some schools can be added, others dropped. It is also time to think about application strategy: Are there any schools to which you would consider applying Early Decision or Early Action? It is also time to adjust your testing plan based on how you did junior year.

October: Focus on essays, first the Common Application Personal Statement. Then attack supplemental essays, such as "Why University of X?" Attend college prep presentations at your high school, and visit a school during fall break.

November–December: Continue the process. Keep up your senior year grades, because colleges will see them.

19. Parents of Eleventh Graders: Get Set for "Junior College Night"

Whatever you do, or dream you can, begin it.

–Johann Wolfgang von Goethe,
Eighteenth C. German writer and polymath

January of junior year. You just got a notice from your eleventh grader's guidance counselor that parents are *strongly* encouraged to attend upcoming "Junior College Night." They want you to know it's time to get serious about your kid's college future.

What to expect? Depends on your school, but most likely it will start off with a preamble on today's college application process, how it dramatically differs from "back in the day." Why, you ask, has the college process become so competitive, and therefore stressful?

Admission Matters: What Students and Parents Need to Know about Getting into College[1] identifies three factors: the "echo" boom (or baby boomlet), social changes, and the Internet.

1. The "echo" boom. The authors state: "More high school graduates than ever are competing for seats in the freshman class...In 1997, there were 2.6 million graduates...by 2009, the number of high school graduates had grown to 3.3 million...they are projected to stay at or above 3.2 million at least until 2022."[2]

The 1990's population explosion explains, at the simplest level, why you were accepted at "Ivy U," but despite playing Mozart in the womb and sending your child to the best prep schools, he or she may be edged out of yesterday's most prestigious colleges. What you viewed as "second tier" may be regarded as a great accomplishment today.

2. Social changes. "A college education is increasingly seen as the key to economic success in our society, just as a high school diploma was once the minimum requirement...At the same time, colleges themselves have increased their efforts to attract large, diverse pools of applicants."[3]

3. The Internet. Not only can students research colleges more efficiently than ever via the Web, but online applications such as the Common Application have made it easy to apply to multiple colleges.[4]

Your guidance counselor will undoubtedly mention these factors, to manage expectations. Resist the temptation to shoot the messenger; the college application landscape really has changed since the olden days. The counselor will also offer the comforting news that there are thousands of accredited four-year colleges to dial down the stress-heightening "run for the roses" feeling.

The authors of *Admission Matters* point out, "The crunch that drives the newspaper headlines and the anxiety that afflicts many families at college application time...is limited to about one hundred colleges that attract applicants from all over the country and the world and that are the most selective..."[5]

Expect an overview of the college process in your particular high school. Your guidance counselor may ask you and your teen to fill out questionnaires that will help generate the initial college list, as well as provide input into the all-important counselor recommendation that will accompany every application. If your school is large and counselors are therefore not able to get to know students individually, your input into the counselor recommendation becomes even more crucial, so don't underestimate the significance of this task.

Your student will be asked to create a college list with the help of the guidance counselor, identify teachers as recommenders, and perhaps fill out extracurricular activity forms, depending on what your school requires. As a parent, it will be essential to pay attention to deadlines and help your teen stay on top of the process.

Be thankful for the structures created by your guidance department. Your teenager would rather follow instructions from a guidance counselor rather than from parents right now. Your counselor is playing that neutral third party role, free from the parent-teen emotional baggage. Because many college process tasks and deadlines will be coming from the guidance department, it saves you from having to be the "bad cop." It also helps your son or daughter to see that college requirements are real, not a parent conspiracy intended to torture teenagers.

Even if you intend to use an independent consultant, your guidance counselor is an essential player. He or she is the expert on your high school's system, has built relationships with admissions departments, and has an accurate picture of your school's track record with individual colleges. He or she will write the counselor recommendation and be the liaison between your student and admissions personnel. Get to know your guidance counselor as well as you can, cooperate with his or her requirements, and listen to his or her advice.

As "Junior College Night" comes to a close, it is probably not a good idea to stick around and chat. The most hyper parents will take center stage now, spouting their misguided opinions as though they are somehow experts, raising the blood pressure of anyone who dares remain in the auditorium. This is not healthy for your family. Go out for ice cream and get back to the ranch. Keep doing your homework and follow any blueprint that is helpful, such as this book.

20. College Reading List for Eleventh Grade Parents

Spectacular achievement is always preceded by spectacular preparation.

–Robert H. Schuller,
American televangelist, pastor, and author

While your high school junior prepares for the SATs and works on keeping grades up in challenging courses, what should you be doing to support the college process?

READ.

Keep college discussions to a minimum for now; as a senior, your teen will get sick of the subject soon enough. Just do your homework, to support your adolescent, and be able to answer your teen's questions naturally as they arise.

MY READING LIST

The College Solution: A Guide for Everyone Looking for the Right School at the Right Price by Lynn O'Shaughnessy.[1] The author is a higher education and financial journalist and popular blogger. Her book advises incorporating financial considerations into the college process from the outset.

Admission Matters: What Students and Parents Need to Know about Getting into College by Sally S. Springer, Jon Reider, and Marion R. Franck.[2] The lead author brings expertise as a psychologist, professor, and chancellor emeritus at UC Davis. This book is a commonsense, no-hype, straightforward "how to" guide to every step of the college process.

The Hidden Ivies, Second Edition: 50 Top Colleges—from Amherst to Williams—That Rival the Ivy League by Howard Greene (Greenes' Guides).[3] The classic guidebook by the renowned higher education consultants has finally been expanded and updated.

Colleges that Change Lives: 40 Schools that Will Change the Way You Think about Colleges by Loren Pope.[4] The veteran writer about higher education presents a paradigm of colleges as transformative experiences rather than credentials to collect.

A is for Admission: The Insider's Guide to Getting into the Ivy League and Other Top Colleges by Michele Hernández.[5] The author, a graduate and former admissions officer for Dartmouth, describes unique characteristics of the admissions process of the Ivy League, such as the Academic Index.

Pay for College without Sacrificing Your Retirement: A Guide to Your Financial Future by financial expert Tim Higgins.[6] This book helps to familiarize families with the basics of affording college.

College Match: A Blueprint for Finding the Best School for You by Steven R. Antonoff[7], former dean of students, admissions and financial aid, University of Denver. This book is a great starting point to help juniors figure out what they may want in a college. Instead of "how to get in," this book offers an emotionally healthy approach to help teens clarify what they're looking for.

The College Finder: Choose the School that's Right for You! by Steven R. Antonoff.[8] Essentially a book of lists, this book helps identify colleges where students will get in and fit in. The book's information now appears on the InsideCollege.com Web site.[9]

Hundreds of lists are presented, such as: best schools for a wide range of college majors; best schools for specific sports and extracurricular activities; demographic composition; schools with specific religious, racial, gender, or social orientations; best schools for students with disabilities; hidden gems. *This book itself is a hidden gem!*

Ultimate Guide to Summer Opportunities for Teens: 200 Programs that Prepare You for College Success by Sandra Berger.[10] The author, an expert on gifted students, presents two hundred programs across a wide range of categories, such as academic enrichment, fine arts, math and science, technology, leadership, service, and study abroad.

The Insider's Guide to the Colleges 2011: Students on Campus Tell You What You Really Want to Know, 37th Edition by Yale Daily News Staff.[11] This book offers frank student opinion with a balanced perspective.

Fiske Guide to Colleges 2011 27E by Edward B. Fiske[12], former education editor for the *New York Times*. Fiske's reference book is a must-have for every college-bound family's bookshelf.

21. Preparing for the SAT: "E" for Effort

Success is the sum of small efforts, repeated day in and day out.

–Robert Collier,
American self-help author

"All types of test prep, with the exception of using books or software, significantly improve students' SAT scores, which in turn are a strong predictor of enrollment in college, and selective college enrollment in particular." So write sociological researchers C. Buchmann et al. in their study, "The Myth of Meritocracy? SAT Preparation, College Enrollment, Class and Race in the United States."[1]

The researchers claim: "The SAT and devices used in preparing for it have become a tool of advantaged families to ensure that their children stay ahead in the competition for college admissions." OK, the affluent have an advantage, as usual. So how can these findings help *all* families with college-bound students?

Most families cannot afford a private SAT tutor or SAT class. According to this study, they are simply out of luck, since books and software, the only affordable prep tools available, apparently do not improve scores. Here is where I raise an eyebrow. *Where do individual differences in motivation come into play?*

Buying an SAT book does not an SAT scholar make, just as buying a violin does not ensure virtuosity. The landmark 1993 study by K.A. Ericsson et al., "The Role of Deliberate Practice in the Acquisition of Expert Performance,"[2] determined that in pursuits such as violin, one's best work is preceded by ten years or *ten thousand hours of practice*. As judged by conservatory teachers, the best group of twenty-year-old violinists in Ericsson's study averaged ten thousand hours of deliberate practice over their lives; the next-best averaged seventy-five hundred hours; and the next, five thousand. The "practice makes perfect" hypothesis has been proven in many domains, such as sports, chess, surgery, and business.

For example, the parents of my niece, Laura, could not afford a private tutor or class to help her prepare for the SATs, so they bought an online software program. That did not automatically improve their daughter's SAT scores; *she had to do something*. Laura practiced before she went to bed, on a consistent basis, raising her scores by at least a hundred points. An accomplished dancer and musician, she transferred her life skill of self-disciplined practicing to standardized testing.

Conversely, I have known students whose parents bought SAT workbooks that they never opened, or online programs they never even "logged onto." I have known parents who hired expensive private tutors, but their students never practiced between sessions. Knowing pro bono students who would have truly capitalized on a chance to work with a tutor, this lack of initiative broke my heart. Resources do not help where there is a lack of will. *No surprise, their scores did not improve.*

The SATs indeed assess aptitude, mediated by, yes, socioeconomic status, family structure, race, gender, and factors such as learning, processing, and test-taking style differences. But they also measure something else: *effort.* I would venture to say that one's discipline and motivation is a pretty good predictor of success in college, and in life.

Am I saying don't hire a tutor? *Absolutely not!* As Buchmann et al. showed, tutors and classes help raise SAT scores. I am a big believer in the transformative power of one-on-one coaching. If you can afford it, I cannot think of a better investment than a tutor. In fact, I am amazed at how many parents are willing to spend big bucks on extracurricular activities (lessons, training camps, state-of-the-art equipment), but are far less willing to spring for a tutor.

What I *am* saying is, the drive within an individual to commit to *painstaking, consistent practice* is what will ultimately drive success in any pursuit. Daily workouts. Your encouragement of such work habits in your student will pay off, not just in SAT performance, but also in accomplishments throughout his or her higher education and employment experiences in the future. We are talking about metaskills here, the ability to set a goal and do what it takes every day to meet that goal.

When my son, Eric, was on the high school cross-county team, he ran every day. If he didn't, he knew he would lose his edge. It couldn't just come from his parents or coach. *It had to come from him.* The same is true of academics or preparing for standardized tests.

22. Should I Take the SAT, the ACT, or BOTH?

Of course, some people do go both ways.

–The Scarecrow, *The Wizard of Oz*
1939 film adaptation of L. Frank Baum's classic book

Standardized testing for college can be overwhelming. Although I am a college consultant and not an admissions testing tutor, parents frequently confront me with the question: "Should my kid take the SAT, the ACT, or *both?*"

Let's see if I can demystify this a little.

1. SAT I Reasoning Test is published by the College Board.[1] Broad brush, this test is considered to be more geared toward critical thinking or reasoning ability. It is usually viewed as the "trickier" of the two tests. The current SAT I Reasoning Test (2005) takes three hours and forty-five minutes. Possible scores range from 600 to 2,400, combining test results from three 800-point sections (Math, Critical Reading, and Writing).

2. ACT Achievement Test is published by ACT, Inc.[2] Broad brush, this test is considered more curriculum-based. It is viewed as the more straightforward test, but one that requires moving at a faster pace. The current ACT Test (2005) consists of four tests: English, Math, Reading, and Science reasoning, with an optional Writing section. It takes two hours and fifty-five minutes, with thirty minutes for Writing. The main four tests are scored individually on a scale of 1-36. The composite is the average of the four scores.

Key Differences:

The two tests differ slightly in *content*.[3] The SAT emphasizes vocabulary, while the ACT stresses grammar and punctuation. Only the ACT has a Science section, assessing the ability to decipher charts, research, and conflicting scientific viewpoints. Only the ACT covers trigonometry.

Structural differences[4]: The ACT has all multiple-choice questions (except Writing), whereas the SAT also requires students to produce answers to math questions. SAT questions become more difficult as the test progresses; the level of difficulty remains constant on the ACT.

The ACT has 215 questions and the SAT has 140. Since both are about three hours long, students have less average time per question on the ACT, requiring that the student move along at a faster clip than on the SAT.

The two tests require different test-taking *strategies*.[5] Students taking the SAT are penalized slightly for wrong answers, so it is wise to eliminate one or two answers and then make the best guess from the remaining choices. ACT test takers are not penalized for wrong answers. Before time runs out, students should guess on any questions about which they are unsure.

The SAT is riddled with questions designed to slow down the test taker. Professional test strategists suggest moving on to the easier questions and coming back to the harder ones.

So...how do you determine which test is right for your high school student? If your teen is a junior, he or she has already essentially taken the SAT *twice*, because in most schools, the PSAT is given in October in the tenth and eleventh grades. The SAT and PSAT are so similar that your kid already *knows* how he or she feels about the SAT. It is important to study for the PSAT because then it provides a relatively accurate gauge of how the student will do on the SAT.

You will get the results of the eleventh grade PSAT by December. If you are disappointed, register for the ACT in February, with in-person tutoring if you can afford it, or at minimum studying online or from a prep book.

By the end of February, you will know which test is the way to go. Compare SAT vs. ACT scores by looking at Internet concordance charts. Your teen will then either sign up to take the ACT again to slightly improve, or abandon ACT and go SAT all the way.

All US colleges now accept both the SAT and ACT. Both testing services now allow you to decide which *test dates* (not sections) you do and do not wish to send to schools. Some colleges that still require SAT II Subject Tests waive that requirement if a student takes the ACT with Writing.

If your student struggles with learning disabilities or attention disorders that may require extra time accommodation, schedule testing with an independent learning consultant who can provide documentation to send to College Board or ACT, Inc., at least six months in advance. Time accommodation is available for both the SAT and ACT (anecdotally, it seems more difficult for the ACT). In either case, it is essential that parents stay on top of the timeline.

23. High School Juniors Apathetic About College Applications?

Nothing is so fatiguing as the eternal hanging on of an uncompleted task.

–William James,
Nineteenth C. American psychologist and philosopher

I often hear parents lament that their high school juniors have not yet gotten "fire in the gut" about college. "Is this normal?" they ask. "Will it *ever* change?" Every student is different, but many still appear apathetic even in the spring of junior year. *Why?* What can you as a parent do about it?

We are dealing with adolescents. Your kid is not an MBA planning machine, obsessing about where he or she will be in five years. In *The Primal Teen: What the New Discoveries about the Teenage Brain Tell Us about Our Kids* [1], author Barbara Starch warns that the prefrontal cortex, the "executive function" brain center that enables us to plan, is not fully formed until we are in our early twenties.

This fact has myriad implications for understanding teen behavior, certainly assessment of risk and consequences of actions. It also suggests that your teenager might not be developmentally ready to focus and plan for the educational future in the way you might expect. *At least not at this moment*—your adolescent is constantly evolving.

Add to this everything else we know about teens and the roller-coaster ride they are constantly experiencing. Physiological, emotional, sexual, social, and physical changes. Peer pressure. First dating relationship—or a devastating breakup. Managing an increasingly rigorous course load along with demanding extracurricular activities. Family issues such as unemployment, sibling conflict, illness, or divorce. Psychological problems like teen depression or eating disorders. Learning disabilities. Substance abuse crises. The list goes on—but *college is clearly not the only thing on your kid's mind.*

What to do? **First, do no harm.** Your teen's responses to your suggestions to visit campuses or research schools for the college list will tell you what he or she is ready for. You know better than to lecture, nag, or make comparisons. *Simply back off* and circle back in a month: your teen's readiness is ever evolving.

You don't want to so poison the relationship with your son or daughter that cooperation becomes impossible senior year, when it is even more crucial for college applications. Your teen is legitimately struggling with autonomy versus approval and, hopefully, the college process will not become the focus of that conflict. Allow your kid to assert independence in nonessential areas, so that a resentful, rebellious attitude does not find its way into college choice.

Sometimes what appears to be passive-aggressive rebellion is actually procrastination as a defense against fear of the unknown, the intruding future that threatens to disrupt their "in the now" world. How scary to imagine that their high school life isn't going to go on forever! If other families or students are beginning to stress out about the college process, your student may also be feigning indifference to block out the hype.

Remember the power of peers. This is Adolescence 101. They are interested in what their friends are "into." Hopefully, you have laid a foundation for a constructive peer group by choosing the community in which they go to public school, enrolling in an independent school, or guiding their choices of friends through the years. Now that investment will pay off, because their peers will soon be talking about the college process. By next fall, it will become progressively more important to them all.

Meanwhile, do your homework. Nothing stops *you* from becoming knowledgeable about the college process, so you can provide guidance when your teen is ready. Peruse some of the books suggested in chapter twenty. Knowledge is power, and becoming well versed in the college process will lower your own anxiety level, give you a sense of confidence and calm, and lay a strong foundation for supporting your son or daughter.

And have a little faith.

24. "I'll Only Visit Colleges I Get Into"

Delay is the deadliest form of denial.

–Cyril Northcote Parkinson,
British naval historian and author

Junior year is winding down, and your teen is exhausted after keeping grades up, taking standardized tests, and pursuing a spring varsity sport. College is still a remote, foggy concept, and your student pushes you away when you suggest visiting a few campuses this summer.

It's tempting to let your son or daughter off the hook. After all, the kid is busy, and maybe just trying to edit back on activities. And you're seeing good academic performance. If you push the college visit thing, you might create conflict and turn your teen off to the college process. Plus, you're pretty overextended yourself, with professional, parenting, volunteering, and eldercare responsibilities. How will you be able to fit in visiting eight to ten campuses too?

Somehow you've got to make it happen. Here's why:

1. College is where your adolescent will spend four of the most formative years of life. In the undergraduate years, a young person will choose a career, perhaps a spouse, and a region of the country to live in. Doesn't it make sense to choose that environment thoughtfully, with not only information but also firsthand exposure?

College visits cannot be crammed into a period of one to two months after an applicant receives an acceptance letter. High school students need six to nine months of visiting, because it *takes time* for their viewpoints and emotional reactions to campuses *to unfold.* College selection should not be a whirlwind courtship in April; rather, it should be the result of long-term "dating" and determining a good match.

2. College is a major financial investment that deserves optimal research, including visiting with enough time to digest the experience. You are about to shell out as much as $200K (for a private college), *one of the largest investments you will ever make.*

If you were planning to purchase a house, would you make an offer based on what you read on the Internet, saying, "If they accept my offer, *then* I'll visit the house during attorney review"? *Of course not!* That wouldn't leave enough time to "sleep on it" and reflect about whether the house is a good "fit" for your family's needs. You'd be under too much time pressure. But waiting until senior year spring to see campuses is almost as foolish.

3. Mistakes are costly. I have heard families rationalize procrastination of college visits by saying, "If he doesn't like it, he can always transfer." Yes, that's true. But having to "start over" at a new campus can be emotionally challenging. Key bonding experiences, such as outdoor orientation, freshman dorm, freshman seminars, and fraternity or sorority rush, take place in the first year. After missing these experiences, it is often more difficult for a transfer student to fit in and have a sense of belonging.

Your student may end up transferring no matter how much upfront research is done on the original school. A young adult is an evolving work in progress. Interests change, sometimes requiring program or school transfers. Social needs change (e.g., a freshman may love a small school close to home, but later "outgrow" the school and want a larger institution). All valid reasons to change. Transferring is not uncommon; the *New York Times* reports that one in three students enrolled in two- or four-year college programs transfer.[1]

But *why set your kid up* for having to go through the disruptive, stressful experience of transferring by allowing procrastination of thorough, timely, hands-on research of schools during the junior and senior years of high school? Remember the old saying, "Get it right the first time." While not always possible, it's certainly a desirable goal.

4. Visiting the college is frequently a factor in gaining acceptance. Many elite colleges require or recommend on-campus interviews, albeit with the option of an interview with an alumnus in your region if you live far away and/or the cost of traveling to campus is prohibitive. As I have often mentioned in this book, *demonstrated interest* in a college has become a key factor in the admissions decision. The rising significance of demonstrated interest is well articulated in the *Boston Globe* article, "A new factor in making that college—loving it."[2]

If you take the time to research a school's programs and visit the campus, communicating how you determined your fit with the school through essays, admissions people will know you are serious. They will surmise that if they accept you, the likelihood of your enrollment is high.

So it's time to start touring colleges. Plan out a reasonable schedule for campus visits, beginning the second semester of junior year.

25. The Next Six Months of College Visits

Let your heart guide you.
It whispers, so listen carefully.

–Little Foot's Mother, *The Land Before Time,*
Animated film by D. Bluth, S. Spielberg, and G. Lucas

You took your high school junior to visit a campus over President's Day, and you hit another one over spring break. But your student did not like either school. Or perhaps your teen's interests are changing so fast that your college list is a moving target. Will you still have time to visit colleges before applying?

The short answer is *yes, but you need to get organized,* anticipating key time windows. It is a good idea to check the colleges' Web sites for visit calendars, to make sure information sessions and tours are scheduled when you want to visit. Most schools require preregistration for info sessions. Here are a few tips on key timeframes:

April is fine, especially if your high school allows kids to take a day off for college visits. Most colleges have information sessions and tours on Saturdays as well, so check the "visit" pages of their Web sites. Be aware colleges are also having "accepted student" events during this time. These events may affect "prospective student" information sessions and tours, as well as lodging availability.

Avoid May. Not only will your student be in the midst of AP, IB, or SAT tests, but also colleges will be having final exams and commencement. There is typically a break in admissions events in early May.

June is OK. After your student is finished with SAT or ACT tests or final exams in June, plan college visits. There will be *some* students around—undergraduates taking summer courses and graduate students doing research. It is not as ideal as visiting during the traditional school year, but your teen can at least get the feel of the campus, decide whether to rule out the school or learn more. If your kid really loves the school, plan to visit again next fall to get the full picture.

July to mid-August is suboptimal. If this is the only window you have, and the college is offering information sessions and campus tours, by all means, take advantage of the time. But there won't be many students around. The *ghost-town* campus doesn't help your teen visualize living among the student body. The weather will certainly not be representative of the campus during the school year. If a school is still under consideration after a summer visit, plan to go again next fall to "kick the tires" under more realistic conditions.

I recommend your student spend the summer in a more valuable way by filling out the Common Application (goes online August 1) and writing college essays.

End of August is a hidden gem. Don't go to the shore that week; go to the campus. Colleges are filled with students, alive with the electric anticipation of a new school year. Orientation programs are in full swing, with activity fairs and friendly kids everywhere. School spirit is high. Admissions is sponsoring info sessions and tours as well.

September weekends are great. Before senior year academics get too overwhelming, hit nearby colleges' information sessions and tours. Your student will get the whole enchilada of what the campus is like with a full student community kicking off the fall semester! If your student is considering applying Early

Action or Early Decision, this is probably the last window for pre-application visits.

Once your student's senior year is in full throttle, with standardized testing in October, it will become difficult to visit schools. Columbus Day weekend is probably the only realistic autumn window. Senior year fall is a critical time to boost scores, grades, and, of course, complete applications.

26. Tips for College Trips

You can observe a lot just by watching.

-Yogi Berra,
American MLB player and manager

I just got back from a whirlwind tour of Mid-Atlantic colleges, accompanying a good friend and her daughter, a rising high school senior. On the drive back, the three of us made a list of ideas that would make campus tours less painful and more productive for college-bound teens. My friend's articulate daughter made some especially insightful suggestions—worth a listen!

Wait for your teen to absorb the experience and express an opinion before you give yours. If you speak first, you will inhibit your student from either forming an impression or expressing it. Your adolescent may emulate your point of view or rebel, depending on your relationship dynamics. Either way, *it won't be his or her own.* Who is getting ready to go to college, anyway? *You already had your chance!*

One key benefit of this experience is your student's discovery of how to combine subjective emotional impressions with rational data and make decisions. Don't deprive your teen of that experience by "jumping the gun" and blurting yours out first.

Don't embarrass your teen by questions you ask in public. This is such an obvious point one would think it need not be mentioned. But during these campus visit days, we saw the inflammatory scenario play out time and again: Show-off Dad doesn't listen to tour guide, and then asks questions the tour guide has just answered. Teenage daughter cringes. Dad doesn't get it: this isn't *his* gig. Parent-teen dynamics can become a distraction, and get in the way of the teen's need to focus on the key question, *"Can I picture myself here for four years?"*

Ask subjective questions of the tour guide. In a natural way, without putting the tour guide on the spot, ask questions that elicit a genuine response. Rather than asking factual questions like "What is undergraduate enrollment?" ask, "How does the school's size feel for you?" or "How do you like living in this college town?"

Practice the art of observation. Encourage your teen to play the role of an anthropologist. Grab a meal at an eatery on campus. Look, listen, and get a feel for the atmosphere. How are students dressed: preppie, hippie, Goth, Bohemian, All-American? What are they talking about? Are the kids ethnically and racially diverse, or do they all look alike? Do they appear connected, warm, and enthusiastic, or do they strike you as isolated, jaded, and overly serious? Do they seem like the kind of people your teen would enjoy "hanging out with"? Check out bulletin boards and student newspaper. What seems to be the focus here? Political activism? Local community? Sports? Greek life? Parties? Clubbing? Campus performing arts events? Graduate or professional school? Commuting? Internships? Future careers?

Use your GPS or Map quest, not the college Web site's directions. Remember the old saw about meeting the realtor at the house, rather than driving there together? This way you can explore, to get an accurate picture of the neighborhood, not just what the realtor wants you to see. We discovered by accident (we got lost!) that the Web site may lead you through the loveliest, safest part of a community, but not give you a full picture of the school's surrounding neighborhoods.

What social, cultural, transportation and shopping resources are nearby? These considerations are especially important if the school is in a remote rural or small suburban location. Is there a lively main street in the town, with restaurants and shops within walking distance? Are there shuttles for getting home safely at night? Are there big box stores around for outfitting dorms and apartments? If the college boasts its proximity to a cosmopolitan city, is there a convenient way to get there?

If your son or daughter gives the school a "thumbs-down," accept the verdict and ask for reasons. A teen must be able to articulate why a specific college is *not* appealing, just as much as why it *is* appealing. This helps the adolescent form decision benchmarks, against which future choices can be measured. Don't try to change your teen's mind if he or she doesn't like a school. Your teen is learning to listen to him or herself, a good thing to be sure.

Make it fun. To state the obvious, *try not to make it onerous!* If you need to bring younger siblings, tie it into a family weekend in the area. Visit a place nearby that's fun for all ages. School Web sites list local attractions, along with lodging and restaurants. I have often heard stories of a kid falling in love with a college while accompanying an older sibling on a family campus visit; the younger sibling sometimes ends up actually attending that college.

Another approach is NO siblings, especially if they don't get along. Family conflict will only distract your junior from the main focus, visualizing that campus as a possible future home. Let your teen bring a friend looking at the same colleges, or go with another family. We've done it, and it makes campus visits bearable for teens—anything is better than being alone with their parents.

If you make it fun, then even if your student does not love the school or ultimately does not gain acceptance, it can still be a pleasant memory of a family outing. The time is coming when you will not be going on many more trips together.

Remember, it's an evolving process. The college process is center stage in your family's life for about a year. Your teen's feelings will change over the course of that year. A college that was ruled out at first may be reconsidered later. It's a moving target, and it should be.

For that reason, college visits should also be spread out (junior spring break, summer, senior fall), so that each set of visits can be absorbed within the context of her evolving sense of what your teen is looking for in a college. If your teen has had enough, take a break for a while. The next time you visit a school, your child will be able to observe with fresh eyes and more maturity.

27. Finding the Best College for Your Major

*It's a helluva start, being able to recognize
what makes you happy.*

–Lucille Ball,
American comedian, model, and actress

"My son is interested in sports marketing," the father explains when I pick up the "Batphone" at Position U 4 College. "What colleges have that major?"

I grab my dog-eared copy of *The College Finder: Choose the School that's Right for You!* [1] by Steven R. Antonoff. Although all the incredible lists from this book are now also offered on the InsideCollege.com Web site,[2] I prefer my beloved paperback that sits on my desk, with all my yellow highlighting and scribbled notes. My favorite section is Majors A to Z.

The College Finder does not list all the colleges offering every possible major, like College Board's comprehensive, gargantuan *Book of Majors 2011.*[3] Instead, it tells you which colleges are considered to have strength in a particular major, based on Dr. Antonoff's discussions with college experts throughout the country.

Book of Majors is also a valuable resource, especially since *The College Finder* does not cover every area of study. *Book of Majors* can be used indirectly to find out how strong a given college is in a specific major. For example, let us say you are interested in identifying universities with "deep" foreign language departments.

Schools that offer rarer majors like Arabic, Persian, Hindi, Mandarin, and Gaelic, not just Spanish or French, are probably a good bet.

There are several college guides on the market devoted to specific fields of study. For teens focused on the arts, I would suggest *Creative Colleges: A Guide for Student Actors, Artists, Dancers, Musicians, and Writers* by Elaina Loveland[4] and *A Guide to College Choices for the Performing and Visual Arts* by Ed Schoenberg and Kevin Buck.[5]

US News and World Report[6] rankings can also help identify schools that belong on the radar screen for specific professional fields, such as undergraduate business and engineering.

Professional organizations' publications and Web sites offer undergraduate program rankings for their fields. For example, *DesignIntelligence*[7] ranks undergraduate and graduate architecture programs based on practitioner surveys. *Architect Magazine*[8] also ranks top programs.

Informational interviewing is another rich resource for identifying the best schools for a specific field of interest. Encourage your son or daughter to talk to adult friends of the family who have pursued similar fields. Your teen can ask what schools they attended, what schools they recommend for this field, what advanced training is necessary to be successful, and what the long-term frustrations and rewards of this career have been for them. Not only will your student find out specific information; he or she will begin to develop the skill of networking to forge a career path. The more your teen researches a career personally, the more he or she will develop a sense of career ownership.

Does your high school student have to choose a major before applying to college? No. There is no stigma to applying "Undecided." However, if your son or daughter can identify a major interest area and select schools for the college list that offer excellent programs in that interest area, then he or she will be that much more ahead of the game. For example, if your student is a talented visual artist, he or she does not have to restrict academic options up front by only considering arts institutes. However, it would be a shame to end up in a small liberal arts school that has such a limited studio arts program that the student needs to transfer if deciding to become an art major. Smart contingency planning can prevent such mismatches.

Two rules of thumb would be: Don't limit options too early, but don't choose a college that doesn't offer the obvious alternatives your student might like to have given his or her interest areas. If your student has an interest in marine biology, it would be a good idea to choose schools that are near a large body of water, offering marine science specialty programs. If your teen is an actor, it would be wise to consider schools with theater programs, located in a cosmopolitan location that would offer acting experience outside of school.

You're getting ready to spend several hundred thousand dollars. Research and planning to find educational programs to support likely majors, based on your student's interest areas, seems like only common sense.

28. Prepare for College Essays by Journaling

Writing is thinking on paper.

−William Zinsser,
American writer, editor, literary critic, and teacher

How can you prepare your high school junior for the college process ahead...especially those *dreaded essays?*

What if your teen is a brilliant mathematician, but has no knack for the written word? Or a creative writing whiz whose talent cannot be channeled into a practical activity like college essays? What about the painful push-pull of high-achieving parents versus a sullen, procrastinating teen, vying for autonomy through passive-aggressive behavior?

In a recent *New York Times* article, "The Almighty Essay,"[1] journalist Trip Gabriel asks insightfully, "What if, like most seventeen-year-olds, a high school senior sounds wooden or pretentious or thunderously trite when trying to express himself in the first person? Prose in which an author's voice emerges through layers of perfectly correct sentences is the hardest kind of writing there is. Plenty of professional authors can't manage it. How reasonable is it to expect of teenagers?"

It is an understatement to suggest that your student needs writing practice, much more than offered in high school. As the *New York Times* journalist rightly points out, your student needs experience in a specific kind of writing: *writing about self.*

Writing about self could encompass: struggle with the big questions; reflections on ordinary experiences; biographical "memoir" storytelling; expressions of anger, love, grief, or quest for justice in response to real situations; or personal views and feelings portrayed through an artistic medium such as poetry.

How can a student be expected to have a "voice" in college essays, if he or she has never "tried out" a voice before? I suggest a student start keeping a *journal*. Magazines in the grocery store encourage adults to keep a journal for catharsis, processing of challenging life events, reduction of stress, and living from a deeper, more authentically connected, spiritual place. So why not teenagers?

Teens are continually experiencing profound and complex inner activity (physiologically, intellectually, sexually, psychologically, and spiritually). Don't you remember adolescence as one of the most difficult times in your life? We often refer to it as a crucible, roller-coaster, or wild ride over white rapids. Journaling can help a teenager navigate stormy upheaval with more inner grounding and direction.

My son, Eric, was always a philosophical thinker, and he asked all the big questions during his adolescence. He was fortunate to be supported by a high school seminar-style philosophy course, which offered a venue for exchanging ideas about consciousness, human nature, good and evil, God's existence, or the meaning of life with like-minded young people. However, Eric frequently wanted to work out things for himself. My husband gave him a little moleskin notebook that he called his "Thought Book." There he recorded any issues with which he was privately wrestling, jotting down possible ideas for resolution.

"Writing is thinking." My son's journaling experience developed his "writing and thinking muscles," indirectly leading to high grades on philosophy and humanities papers. More importantly, however, it brought him more in touch with who he was as a human being. College essays flowed out naturally after years of keeping a "Thought Book."

Suggest journaling to your adolescent. It may not be as philosophical as my son's "Thought Book." It may be a travelogue about family summer trips. Or a diary describing everyday occurrences, with feelings about those events. Or an Internet blog (with good judgment about what to share publicly).

Practice makes perfect, but writing is so therapeutic and good for the soul that a young person may not even realize that he or she is "practicing." Not only will college essays be easier, but decisions will be easier too. Your evolving young adult will become more grounded, and authentically in touch with that all-important "inner voice."

29. Teachers' Recommendations

*Successful people turn everyone who can help them
into sometime mentors!*

–John Crosby,
American columnist and media critic

When should your high school junior begin the process of soliciting teachers' recommendations for college, who are the ideal teachers to ask, and how should your student go about it?

When? Believe it or not, **NOW.** Before the end of junior year. Your high school guidance counselor may not be officially asking students to do that yet. However, put yourself in the position of a teacher, who will be deluged with requests next fall. Especially the "living legend" teachers that *everybody* wants to ask. That teacher will be stressed out, writing about each student fast and furiously, perhaps with quality sacrificed in the process.

But what if that teacher was able to work on your kid's recommendation over the summer? Not only would the teacher be appreciative of the extra time, but also he or she might spend more time thoughtfully reflecting on how to effectively write about your teen's attributes.

Who? The conventional wisdom is, two eleventh grade teachers of "solids": math, science, English, history, or language. Admissions people are interested in the up-to-the-minute development of an applicant. So a teacher who has known the student *very* recently can offer more valuable commentary than a teacher from a few years ago. Adolescents change quickly, and admissions people want the most recent snapshot possible.

Yes, there are exceptions. My son had a mentor-like teacher who had taught him AP History in tenth grade and IB Economics in twelfth grade, keeping touch with him during the year in between. He also wrote brilliantly and had keen human insights, a terrific choice for a recommender.

What if an arts elective teacher knows your child well, and your child is planning to major in the arts? Must recommenders be teachers of "solids," then? It depends. If the student is applying to an arts institute, conservatory, or bachelor of fine arts program, one teacher could be an arts teacher. If the applicant is going the liberal arts route with interest in the arts but is not committed to becoming an arts major, it is best to have two "solids" recommenders and an additional "arts" recommender, such as a drama director, attached to the Common Application Arts Supplement.

Must one recommender be math or science, and one be English or humanities? I do not make this stipulation with my clients. In my view, it is more crucial that the teacher know the student well, be a persuasive writer, and that the recommendation *leaps off the page*. Generally, an English teacher is likely to be a better writer than a math teacher. It makes no sense to "force" a lackluster math recommendation when a humanities teacher's writing could make the applicant shine. If your kid is an Einstein who happens to have a math teacher who is gifted at describing the mathematical creativity of his or her star students, by all means ask that teacher. But generally, SATs and grades in math courses probably provide the best measure of a student's quantitative chops.

How? Requests for recommendations must always be first done in person, by the student, *not* the parent. The student needs to elicit an honest response by asking, "I would be honored if you would write a recommendation for my college applications. Do you feel positively enough about my performance in your class to write a positive recommendation?"

If the teacher hesitates, and does not appear comfortable saying yes, that is not a good sign. A halfhearted recommendation will not serve the applicant well. If the vibes are not enthusiastic, the applicant should bow out gracefully and seek a different recommender.

If the teacher agrees wholeheartedly, the student should follow up in writing. I am a believer in giving recommenders all the ammunition they need. Your student's teacher may not be aware of everything he or she does in and out of the classroom. Teachers do not have perfect memories. Your student's teacher may not recall every wonderful paper or project your kid aced while taking the teacher's course. I suggest that the applicant follow up the verbal request with written material (e-mail is fine, since this is how students communicate with teachers today). Attach a resume, activity list, or reference the student's Web site if the student has a visual arts portfolio or recordings of theater performances.

The teacher's role is to describe direct experience with the student, but a cover letter and resume suggest a "big picture" perspective of what the student is all about. Some high schools actually have students fill out forms to help "jog the teacher's memory," giving the student more opportunity to "own the narrative." If your high school uses such a form, attach it to the request for recommendation as well.

The resume gives input, but of course, the teacher's job is to offer more "flesh-and-blood" perspective to make the application come alive. Hopefully, the teacher will have sufficient memory of classroom examples to add that touch. A cover letter can offer reminders, upon which your recommender can expand. Below are two typical examples:

"Your American history class really helped me learn how to organize and prepare a major research paper. My paper on *The Roaring Twenties* helped me learn how to use primary sources and analyze societal trends." The student should attach a copy of the paper, scanned with the grade and comments from the teacher. The attached paper should immediately jog the teacher's memory about the student's contributions to that class.

"Your AP government course made politics come alive for me. Participating in the in-class debates made me realize I had a gift for public speaking. As a result, I joined our high school forensics team and mock trial club. I plan to do Model Congress next year. I am considering majoring in political science in college." The student has connected the outside activities listed on the resume with the influence of the teacher in the government class. This integration is not only gratifying for the teacher, but gives the teacher a broader perspective of the student and his or her long-term goals.

A word of caution. Your student is *not* telling the teacher what to write. It is not appropriate to try to put words in a recommender's mouth. It is desirable, however, to provide information that can help the teacher write a powerful recommendation with good examples.

Finally, the Common Application Teacher Recommendation form has a signature statement by which the student can decide to waive the right to see the recommendation. It is advisable to *waive the right*. This way, admissions knows that the teacher had the freedom to write whatever professional judgment dictated, without pressure.

P.S. Remind your teen to send a thank you note next year after it's all over (an email is fine). The teacher will appreciate being kept in the loop about where your student ends up going to college. Keeping in touch is always a good thing.

V. Senior Year of High School

30. Tricks and Treats of the Common Application

Knowing is not enough. We must apply.

−Leonardo da Vinci,
Fifteenth C. Italian polymath

Halloween has always been my favorite holiday. Trying on different identities so arouses the imagination. My sister and I used to show off our flair for the theatrical by creating homemade costumes in the "olden days" before Party City.

As Halloween approaches, I am busily helping seniors meet November Early Decision and Early Action deadlines. *That's pretty scary!* And the Common Application is so full of "Tricks and Treats" that I thought I would share a few.

For the uninitiated, the Common Application[1] is a form applicants use (online or paper via mail) to apply to over four hundred member colleges and universities. Members are committed to the premise of *holistic admissions*, using subjective criteria such as essays and recommendations alongside objective criteria like grades and test scores.

The "Common App," as it is affectionately called, requires one personal statement essay in response to one of five prompts or topic of your choice, which needs to be an uploaded document of at least 250 words. I usually suggest the personal choice topic, since it offers the most flexibility to reveal oneself directly. Only an exceptional writer can use an essay about a book or a historical figure to *indirectly* self-reveal. The personal statement is an opportunity to "bring the whole application together" in a meaningful narrative, fill in gaps that the form doesn't address, and speak in one's own authentic voice.

Common App also requires a short answer, maximum of 150 words, to be cut-and-pasted into the response space, asking the applicant to elaborate on one especially meaningful extracurricular activity. I advise choosing an activity that you intend to pursue in college, which will contribute to campus life in a major way.

Remember, the college process is more than just a self-discovery exercise. It is a chance for your student to communicate to colleges the unique benefits she brings to campus. *What's in it for them* to admit your kid? Your student's Chia pet collection is probably not going to do much to enrich campus life. However, a passion for starting dance marathons to cure cancer is bound to enrich the college community. Or an enthusiasm for joining the orchestra, choral ensemble, or club sports.

What about the "additional information" prompt? If your student has no extenuating circumstances to explain, I recommend uploading a resume. Yes, your teen has already filled in extracurricular activities. But the resume allows the applicant to "own the narrative" and position one's credentials in a distinctive, themed way.

If your student has extenuating circumstances, such as a serious illness that negatively affected grades, by all means the student should explain it. This is not a confessional ploy for pity. It is a factual explanation that will overcome obstacles to his or her candidacy. The explanation should be truthful and straightforward (no drama), and should specify what your teen did to turn the situation around.

Your student need not worry about the potential stigma of needing medication or testing accommodations for a diagnosed injury, illness, or learning disability. Without explanation, a severe grade drop is certainly *more* damaging to his or her candidacy. In the case of a psychological condition, my advice would be based on the individual situation. Sort this out with your teen's guidance counselor and mental health professional.

One little Common App "trick" to remember. When asked to fill out the dreaded activity list, with hours per week and weeks per year, keep in mind they are asking to list activities in *order of importance* to the student. But your teen should avoid listing activities willy-nilly, expecting to be able to change the order at the end. The Common App is a brilliant program, but has not yet added an "organize" feature. It will save frustration to write out activities on a separate sheet of paper, figure out an order, and then enter them into the online program. And don't forget to *save*, because the Common App closes out after periods of inactivity.

Halloween gives us permission to try on different identities. Turns out, so does the Common App. We simply plug in a bunch of colleges, and this one application efficiently facilitates the opportunity for any number of possible acceptances and the accompanying life trajectories. Then are we done? No, *there's a trick!* Member colleges can require their own supplements, which frequently include additional essays. The most common essay prompt for a supplemental application is, "Why University of X?"

Before responding, your student should go to the college's Web site and thoroughly research its mission, academic programs, and extracurricular offerings. The purpose of this question is to identify the applicants who are seriously interested in the school, certainly enough to explore the Web site.

Recall that the *NACAC State of College Admission 2010 Report*[2] shows that *demonstrated interest* is "of considerable importance" in admissions decisions for 21 percent of colleges. So when responding to the "Why University of X?" prompt, your student should give some evidence that he or she actually knows something about the school. Your student needs to prove that he or she can see the match between the school's offerings and his or her credentials and goals. Encourage your student to take the time to do this. It will help your teen stand out, because you would be surprised at how many applicants don't even bother.

And for God's sake, when using any boilerplate paragraphs for more than one school, your student needs to remember to change the name of the college as appropriate! Admissions readers love to tell war stories about applicants who forgot to check their essays for embarrassing mistakes like this.

So that the Common App will be *all treats and no tricks,* encourage your student to print it out and review it thoroughly for spelling, punctuation, and grammar before pressing "Submit." After all, your kid is applying to college.

31. Senior Year Parent? Learn to Paint

When I'm painting, I'm not aware of what I'm doing.

–Jackson Pollock,
American abstract expressionist painter

My sister calls it *"agita."* My Jewish girlfriend used to call it *"shpilkis."* It's the kind of waiting that drives you crazy inside. You feel a sense of urgency, but the action isn't up to you. You feel impotent and absolutely furious, like your head will explode.

"Did you finish that Common App essay yet?" you call out in your friendliest milk-and-cookie voice. However, your sugarcoated nagging does not fool your seventeen-year-old. He has made up his mind to procrastinate, apparently as a passive-aggressive maneuver just to annoy you, as punishment for infringing on his budding autonomy (or, in your *parent-noia*, are you simply imagining this?)

He finally calls your bluff on the friendliness. "Stop it, Mom! I've got homework to do too, you know!" *Which* he isn't even doing yet, even though he's been home from school an hour already. The Xbox sound effects drone on from the den, as if to mock you. *You want to let out a primal scream!* Doesn't he know applying to college is one of the most important actions of his life? Why doesn't he...*JUST DO IT?*

You bite your tongue. You remember what the guidance counselor said about high school seniors "owning" the process. But what are you going to do with all this nervous energy, anxiety about the outcome, and anger about his attitude?

One day I just got in the car, drove to Michael's arts and crafts store, bought a wooden desk easel, a set of acrylics, canvas, brushes, accessories, and an instructional book. I spent a few hundred bucks but I told my husband that it was safer than the Short Hills Mall. I set up at the kitchen breakfast bar, downloaded a collection of New Age Celtic music, slapped some titanium white gesso down on the canvas, and became a painter.

Not necessarily a *good* painter. But it made that glacially slow, nerve-wracking autumn a little more tolerable. "Watching paint dry" didn't seem so torturous when I was actually *painting* (i.e., doing something I could get lost in).

And it made me a *better mother*. When I wasn't breathing down his neck so much, he took more ownership. He finished his essays. He applied to college. Eric did just fine. And *we didn't kill each other in the process!* We actually still like each other.

Later that spring, I emerged from my painting sabbatical with more amateurish creations than room on my shelves, composed with pure joy and beginner's abandon. I was finally ready to "lunch" with the other high school moms again.

I mentioned what I had been doing to detach and survive senior year fall. Another mother piped in, "I can't believe you started painting. I actually learned to crochet when my son was a senior." Yet another added, "I took up knitting. It made the hours fly, and helped me keep my mind off the college process!"

So I wasn't the only one. As you start senior year, pick a new hobby, immerse yourself in it, and give your teen some peace. (Well, do nag *once* in a while).

32. How Important Is the College Essay, Really?

Don't try to figure out what other people want to hear from you; figure out what you have to say. It's the one and only thing you have to offer.

–Barbara Kingsolver,
American novelist, essayist, and poet

For the budding JK Rowlings among us, the best part of the college application process is writing the essay. However, for many high school students, it looms like tomorrow's trip to the oral surgeon to have wisdom teeth removed.

Parents ask me, "How important is the essay, *really?*" That question reflects a cynicism and sense of futility in the face of the competitiveness of the college process. Unfortunately, that jaded attitude may be picked up by their teens. My answer is, *"Very."* Here's why.

The application is a puzzle from which an admissions counselor, like a good detective, tries to put together a picture of *who you are* and what you will uniquely bring to the school. Most puzzle pieces are indirect: GPA, test scores, awards, and activities. There is only one puzzle piece in which you, the applicant, have a direct voice: *the essay.*

It is tempting to believe that with the deluge of applications colleges receive today, driven by the demographic bulge of the baby boomlet and the convenience of the Common Application, essays have become less important than in the past. The truth is just the opposite.

Recall that in the *NACAC State of College Admission 2010 Report*[1], *essays rank fifth*, with 26 percent of all higher education institutions saying the essay is of "considerable importance" in the admissions decision. That percentage has doubled since the survey was first conducted in 1993.

As discussed in chapter three, the relative importance of essays varies based on the type of institution. 31 percent of private institutions give essays "considerable importance," versus only 13 percent of public institutions. We have speculated that this difference is somewhat driven by the admissions staff readers available versus the number of applicants. "Stats" naturally become more important than qualitative measures when there is a need to accommodate large numbers.

Clearly, if your student is applying to a small, private liberal arts college that is test optional, he or she should expect that the essay will be given significant weight. But even if your student is applying to a large state university, the power of the essay should not be discounted. An essay will not be enough to compensate for lackluster grades or test scores for acceptance to a state school, but it may be a tiebreaker if the student is within striking distance of acceptance. At 13 percent, essays still outrank extracurricular activities, which are given "considerable importance" in only 5 percent of public institutions.

Why are essays important to colleges? In a small, private liberal arts college, I believe it is like inviting guests to a small party, or screening potential pledges for a fraternity or sorority. The admissions staff is creating a local community, so getting to know applicants in an intimate, subjective way through an essay or interview is particularly appropriate.

So what about state universities? My instinct is, that in both public and private institutions of higher education, an applicant's ability to communicate clearly via the written word is a vital attribute for success. I say, thank God. This is, after all, college.

Moreover, essays are *always important for the applicant personally.* The essay offers the applicant one of the few opportunities in this pivotal process in his or her young life to *speak directly, in one's own authentic voice.* This is a chance for self-discovery and self-definition. When my clients write about themselves, they clarify who they are. They integrate their experiences within their own interpretive narrative. I cannot think of a more essential exercise for an adolescent and an evolving human being.

33. Does the College Essay Topic Matter?

Be yourself. Above all, let who you are, what you are, what you believe, shine through every sentence you write.

–John Jakes,
American writer of historical fiction

"Don't write a sports essay. Admissions people see so many of those, and they get bored." This pseudo-wise advice is often given to confused high school students, who are desperately trying to figure out a killer topic for their central college application essay.

Why *not* write a sports essay?

Athletics is one of the chief arenas in which adolescents can learn key lessons about leadership, perseverance, mental toughness, discipline, strategy, teamwork, courage, commitment, hard work, and professionalism. (Why else engage in athletics at all?) How can such a huge theater of experience be *off-limits* for college essays?

What's this about being afraid to "bore" admissions readers? *Since when* should it be an applicant's goal to "entertain" an audience? It was always my impression that admissions professionals were interested in young people's development, *what makes them tick*. How, then, can any enormous category of adolescent experience be *verboten* because it might "bore" the readers?

Are admissions officers not mostly young people themselves, enthusiastic, people-oriented, and intrigued by formative experiences of teen applicants? If admissions officers so easily burn out on a specific essay topic so seminal to adolescent development, perhaps they are in the wrong line of work.

It is not the essay *topic* that matters in the end. What matters is how the applicant is using the content area to demonstrate character. In other words: *What does the essay say about YOU?* What did you learn from the situation described in the essay? How could that learning translate into a valuable contribution to campus life?

All elements of an application are communication tools, to paint a comprehensive portrait of the applicant's strengths, passions, and potential contribution to a college. In my practice, I help clients use all those elements to express a student's unique positioning.

In my view, *an essay should complete the picture of the applicant.* It is a final puzzle piece that has not been communicated by other measures in the application (such as activity list, awards, grades, test scores, resume). I feel an essay is a waste of an opportunity if it simply repeats something that is elsewhere reported in the application. *It should not be a romp through one's resume.* It should not repeat academic, athletic, or artistic accomplishments. It should tell the admissions reader something that *has not yet been revealed.*

A proud mother once shared a memorable essay anecdote with me. Her son, an academic star, football standout, and talented musician, wrote an essay about a less salient side of his personality: *vulnerability.* Members of the football team were asked to receive training in dance, to help them develop grace and flexibility on the field.

This young man found dance training to be a humbling experience, from which he learned "beginner's mind," challenging himself in a new area where he had no expertise or natural ability. After this student was admitted to one of the most elite Ivy

League schools in the country, the admissions officer who read his essay commented on how persuasive that self-revelation had been in his candidacy.

Technically, it was a sports essay (with a twist). But it wasn't a self-congratulatory, stereotypic narrative about a touchdown in the last five seconds of a game. It was about *what he learned*, how an experience brought about in a sports training context *changed him*. The context is not the point. It's the learning.

A student's storytelling ability is essential as well. An everyday occurrence can be fascinating in the hands of a creative story-teller. I am not talking about flowery language meant to impress the reader, which can often sound phony, hackneyed, or thesaurus-based. An essay should be conversational storytelling that weaves an engaging tale with a powerful message. Period.

34. "Confessional" College Essays

Never apologize, Mister, it's a sign of weakness.

–John Wayne,
American film actor, director, and producer

Recently, a family returned from a university information session, confused about essay advice offered by the admissions representative. "Avoid the three D's," she recommended. *"Death, Divorce, and Disease."* The advice gave this family the impression that admissions readers are not empathetic. I explained that admissions officers are extremely people-oriented; otherwise, they would not be in this occupation. Why, then, should applicants avoid describing difficult life circumstances in their essays?

The key objective of the personal statement is to communicate the applicant's strengths. If a student chooses to write about a personal hardship, the student must use it to show how he or she responded to the situation, and how it built character, courage, determination, or empathy. The reader must come away from the essay understanding how the applicant will constructively contribute to the college community because of learning gained from that difficult personal struggle.

Adolescents, like all human beings, have a legitimate need for self-expression. It is part of processing our experiences, a key ingredient of self-discovery and development. I am an enthusiastic proponent of all forms of self-expression, such as the arts, journaling, honest sharing in relationships, and psychotherapy. But all private self-expression doesn't need to become public.

The college application is certainly one vehicle of self-expression. If you don't reveal yourself in your application, essays, or resume, you risk being inauthentic. Lack of authenticity not only does a disservice to the institution to which you are applying; it does you the greatest disservice of all.

However, self-expression does not mean *confession*, or as we used to say back in the 1970s, "letting it all hang out." Writing a college essay is indeed a therapeutic process; however, it is *not* psychotherapy. Nor should it be.

When you write the essay, first consider: *who is my target audience?* What is my reader most interested in? Your reader is not a shrink; he or she is an admissions officer. That person's job is to be a gatekeeper, to decide whom to accept and whom to deny acceptance.

Admissions officers are likely to accept an applicant who has overcome obstacles through inner drive. But if a candidate writes only about dysfunctional family dynamics, without evidence of having risen above problems, how does that convince the admissions officer to admit the student?

My husband once worked for a senior executive of a bank in Chicago, who routinely rejected job candidates who indicated any hint of unresolved psychological weaknesses. This tough, cigar-chewing CFO used to say, *"We're not running a rehabilitation center here."* A job interview is not a pity party, and employers do not hire people out of sympathy.

The same could be said for colleges. Admissions people aren't looking for suffering teens to "cure" and set on a path to fulfillment. Rather, they seek young people who have learned from tough situations and are now ready to hit the ground running and make valuable contributions to their college community.

On the darker side of this discussion, no admissions person wants to be the gatekeeper who accepts a deeply troubled individual who ultimately becomes a threat to the student body. With incidents such as the Virginia Tech massacre in our collective recent memory, there is always an underlying fear of another Seung-Hui Cho, and the need to be vigilant to prevent a similar tragedy.

Thus, before submitting a dark, confessional essay, an applicant needs to imagine being in the position of the reader, who does not know the applicant personally. The applicant needs to consider whether the essay might create the impression of a troubled adolescent. I am certainly not suggesting dishonesty; I am simply saying that there is no need to reveal your innermost personal issues to strangers in a college essay.

One exception is when personal circumstances legitimately explain an academic "blip." For example, if an A student suddenly got a C junior year, because the student's father died of cancer, that situation should be clearly explained. The communication is intended to overcome an obstacle to college acceptance. When the low grade is placed in perspective, the admissions officer will weigh it differently than if it just appeared out of the blue with no explanation.

In closing, I would like to share an apt quote from Don Dunbar's *What You Don't Know Can Keep You Out of College*.[1] The admissions gatekeeper has to decide, based on exposure to an applicant through essays or interviews, whether the gatekeeper wants to invite this person to join the college community he or she represents:

"Imagine this: You are asked to pick one of two strangers from the grade below you to spend the night at your house. The kid you pick will eat dinner with your family, use all your things, share your bathroom, and sleep right down the hall. In the morning, you'll go to class together.

"One of these kids is talented and smart and seems responsible. The other one is talented and smart but seems like a selfish, impulsive third grader. Which one do you choose? Oh, and one other thing: Making this choice is your new job, and your family will kick you out if the kids you pick trash your house...Welcome to the perspective of an admissions person."[2]

35. "Why University of X?" College Essay

My most brilliant achievement was my ability to be able to persuade my wife to marry me.

–Sir Winston Churchill,
British prime minister, statesman, and orator

When I work with high school students on this essay, asked in every school-specific supplement to the Common Application, their knee-jerk response is to play back obvious answers. *"I love New York!" "Atlanta has perfect weather!" "Washington, DC is the best place for a poli sci major." "Denver has great skiing." "Boston is the ideal college town."*

Don't get me wrong. Those answers are valid, and they enter into college decisions (and should). But the admissions committee *"gets"* those reasons: they don't even need to be said. So what should your student say?

My consulting practice is called Position U 4 College for a reason. Your student needs to persuade the admissions committee that he or she is *uniquely positioned for their school,* that there is an ideal match between their programs, student body, extracurricular activities, and environment and your student's interests, skill set, goals, values, and personality. Why are your student and College X *made for each other*?

Your student's response to this essay question should reflect two things: (1) your student's *self-knowledge* and (2) well-researched *knowledge of the college* to which your student is applying.

Knowledge of the school's programs is a powerful way to show *demonstrated interest*. We have already discussed how this factor has become significant for admissions people under pressure to maximize their yield and accurately predict enrollment.[1,2] If choosing a college is more like marriage than winning a prize, your student should offer a passionate proposal based on already knowing and loving the school.

If your student takes time to thoroughly research a school's programs, it shows a serious interest in that college. If the match makes sense, evidenced by programs that clearly fit your kid's individual goals, the admissions people will surmise that, if they accept your kid, the likelihood of your enrollment is high.

PS: Your student needs to visit the school and let them *know* about it. To revisit the marriage metaphor: Would anyone ever propose without a date?

Answering this question with well-researched content on programs will set your student apart. Why? Because *most kids won't do this*. They are answering the question superficially, saying what they would say to their friends: "Evanston is a great college town and it's easy to hop the 'L' to Chicago." It would be more effective to write: "Northwestern's Medill School of Journalism is the top journalism school in the country, on the leading edge in new media, so it is the ideal place for me to pursue my journalism major."

Powerful communication means considering your target audience: what will be meaningful to *them*? I don't mean telling them what you believe they want to hear or offering up phony flattery; just consider their *frame of reference*.

"Georgetown has a beautiful campus" does not say what your student is going to contribute to the educational experience if accepted. It would more convincing to say: "Georgetown's political economy major and government minor will help me in my goal to become a lawyer and ultimately a US Supreme Court justice."

Believe me, your student will stand out by taking the time to do a little research and give some substantive reasons for interest in a specific college. Your student may even become more convinced to go there (or *not*). And isn't that what this whole college search is about, anyway?

36. The College Waiting Game

The Waiting...is the hardest part.

-Written by Tom Petty,
American singer-songwriter
Performed by Tom Petty and the Heartbreakers

Thanksgiving is over, and your high school senior returns to school for one of the most nerve-racking periods of an already stressful year. Your high school student may have chosen to apply Early Decision (ED), Early Action (EA), priority application, or rolling admissions. Even if your teen chose Regular Decision, the atmosphere will be wired with contagious tension for *all* seniors during the next few weeks.

For early applicants, the white-knuckle, nail-biting suspense really sets in now. That wilderness of free-floating anxiety and acceptance stress between Thanksgiving and the winter holidays. It is such an all-or-nothing feeling, as though your kid's whole self-worth and future destiny rests on one online message. It starts: *"Congratulations..."* or perhaps something else. You won't need to read the rest.

As a parent, keep it in perspective, and pass on your wisdom to your student. This is *not* an all-or-nothing verdict. Early Decision was a college enrollment invention to guarantee yield, not for families' benefit. This Faustian bargain gives applicants an acceptance advantage and early relief in the tortuous college process, in exchange for losing financial aid package choices and a longer incubation time for college exploration. Early Action was created to help admissions people spread out their workload, sometimes with an acceptance advantage, depending on the school.

Be realistic during this period, and prepare your student for the most likely outcome. Was this university in the realistic range, perhaps a slight reach, for which the early advantage will likely compensate? Or was this school a pipe dream, a "Hail Mary Pass," to which your teen applied early to maximize advantage but still a long shot? You probably already know the answer in your heart.

If it's a long shot, help your student put it on the back burner. Emphasize that it is only one of *many* options. Keep your teen working on essays for Regular Decision schools. If December's decision is disappointing, your kid will not be overwhelmed by consequential application work required over the holidays before January deadlines.

All the schools on your teen's college list need to be genuine, appealing choices, not halfhearted backups. This will mitigate the all-or-nothing feeling about December news. Help your student to take the long view: even if there are short-term disappointments, by April your teen will probably be quite pleased.

Advise your student to keep a low profile. If the news is disappointing, your teen may be uncomfortable keeping up a "game face" with peers, especially those receiving happy news. The opposite is also true. Friendships can become strained, at least temporarily. Try to preserve them for the long haul through empathy, sensitivity, and discretion. Follow this advice yourself with other parents, who often get even more wound up than their kids.

If your student chose not to apply early, what should he or she be doing now? Completing essays and applications. And "pushing the button" as soon as possible. Although Regular Decision applications are not due until January 1 or beyond, it doesn't hurt to get applications and supporting documentation in early. The sooner an application is complete, the sooner it can be reviewed, by readers who are "fresh" at the start of the evaluation process, not overwhelmed and burned out.

37. December College News

There is no failure. Only feedback.

–Robert G. Allen,
American-Canadian financial writer

So, will there be a toy in your stocking or a lump of coal? Let us consider each early admission scenario, with wise input from *Admission Matters: What Students and Parents Need to Know about Getting into College,* by Sally S. Springer, Jon Reider, and Marion R. Franck.[1]

Early Decision (ED): Accepted. *Whew!* Your student is done with the college process, the outcome is positive, and your family can celebrate and relax over the holidays. But wait, you're not done yet. If financial aid is relevant to your child's attendance, you will need to review the aid package.

"Unmet financial need is the only grounds for not attending a college that admits you under binding early decision. If your financial aid package provides less money than you will need to attend, contact the financial aid office immediately…respectfully request that your financial aid package be reviewed…The family makes the final decision about whether the early decision financial aid package is sufficient to allow the student to attend."[2]

If aid is not an issue, your student is honor bound to attend the school. A deposit is required in a few weeks. Your teen must contact every school to which he applied early, and *immediately withdraw his application.* "Some selective colleges using early decision share their acceptance lists as a way to police compliance with the binding policy. If your name were to show up on two early decision admit lists, you would be in trouble with both schools."[3]

Advise your teen to keep the news understated at school. This is a tense time for high school seniors, many gripped by a "life or death" feeling. Most students who are disappointed now end up gratified by April, but this month it may seem like the end of the world to those deferred or denied.

Prepare your ecstatic teenager for unpleasant dynamics, ranging from other kids' egocentric inability to cheer for peers to downright jealousy. Friendships can become strained, even broken off. Encourage your adolescent to be gracious and supportive. Remember, discretion is the better part of valor. And please, *no obnoxious college sweatshirts!*

Early Action (EA): Accepted. *What a happy relief!* If the school is your student's first choice, the process could be over, unless your family needs to compare financial aid packages. If the school offering early acceptance is not your teen's first choice, the process will continue to meet Regular Decision (RD) deadlines.

Either way, a decision and deposit are not required until May 1. But it certainly adds a cushion of comfort to know that your student has a college to attend next fall that is an appealing choice.

If financial aid is not an issue, and the school is truly your student's first choice, should you wait until May 1? It is courteous to send in your deposit, withdrawing applications from other colleges, as soon as you know this is where you will attend. "If you know for sure where you will be going...share your good fortune by giving your fellow students (locally and nationally) a better chance for a regular decision at one of the colleges they would like to attend."[4]

What to do if you're deferred? What does deferral *mean, anyway?* It depends on the school. "Some, like Georgetown University, defer all or most [applicants they do not accept early], denying only those who clearly don't meet the qualifications for admission...Other colleges prefer to make hard decisions sooner rather than later, denying many qualified candidates they know they would deny in the regular cycle anyway, and deferring just a small percentage who look competitive for the final round...If there is a trend, it is in the direction of denying more students in the early round rather than fewer."[5]

Michele Hernández discusses the varying meanings of deferral in *A is for Admission: The Insider's Guide to Getting into the Ivy League and Other Top Colleges* [6]: "...You will not know if you were a polite defer (that is, a valedictorian with low test scores who will probably not be admitted anyway but was deferred to show that he was strong enough not to be rejected outright) or a realistic defer (that is, somebody who looked pretty strong but the college wanted to wait for more scores and/or midyear grades to see how the person performed while carrying a challenging senior year course load)." [7]

Both Springer et al. and Hernández suggest that the applicant call admissions to get a sense of how to improve chances in the regular cycle, write a letter to reaffirm the school as the top choice, add at most one powerful letter of recommendation, and update the school about new awards. And finish the fall term with strong grades! But both authors caution that the odds of a deferred applicant gaining regular admission are not high. [8,9]

Given the low odds of admission after deferral, your twelfth grader should continue to apply regular decision, All schools on this list should be genuine choices, not halfhearted backups. If the deferral decision was a wake-up call that your teen shot too high, *reassess.* Talk to the guidance counselor and utilize quantitative tools, such *Naviance* [10] Family Connection, to re-evaluate the realism of your college list. Add less competitive schools, but institutions your teen would be happy attending.

What to do if you're denied? Most next steps are the same as for deferral. Of course, denial has a more painful sting. Springer et al. point out: "The problem with an early application denial is that it usually occurs in isolation, and also at holiday time...students usually apply early to only one college, and those who receive denials have no simultaneous acceptances to ease the blow." [11]

While it is easier to "save face" with peers when deferred, the finality of denial allows the student to move on. A deferral will most likely not end in eventual acceptance, but since it keeps hope alive, it may result in a halfhearted, less effective application effort for the regular cycle. Denial is a blow, but (after letting off steam) the student is ready to resume the process. Hopefully, you have kept your teen working on Regular Decision essays all along, so he or she will not be totally back at square one.

This may be a difficult experience in your family. Accepted students may not be gracious or supportive. Others who were deferred or denied may ignite a nasty, sour grapes attitude within the senior class.

Advise your adolescent to take the high ground, and model that behavior yourself. Eventually good news will come, but it is now a long four months away. Try to boost your teen's self-esteem, with the reminder that this simply means that the admissions committee of this particular college decided not to admit him or her. This may mean academic credentials were not quite strong enough for this institution, or that the admissions people surmised the match wasn't there, or even random occurrences over which he or she has no control.

Fast forward to the experience of college grads in this economy. I work with young adults who job-hunt for months, often weathering disappointment, learning to be patient in between opportunities, keeping their spirits up until they land the job they want. Learning to postpone gratification is a key life skill. Early admission deferral or denial in grade twelve may be the first time your child has faced this kind of challenge, but it won't be the last. Your teen might as well learn how to survive it with self-esteem intact.

38. Waiting for the "Fat Envelope"

The Waiting Place...everyone is just waiting.

–Theodor Geisel (Dr. Seuss),
American cartoonist and writer of children's books

Unless your high school student was accepted to his or her first choice college through an early action program, your family is still playing the college waiting game this spring. Some universities, particularly public schools, notify by the middle of March, giving the term "March Madness" a whole new meaning. But the final information, including many colleges' notification, merit awards and need-based financial aid packages, arrives around April first (yes, that's right, *April Fool's Day!*). Enrollment deposits are universally due on May first.

This waiting game has pros and cons compared to the early notification wait in December. The early wait has a white-knuckle, all-or-nothing feel to it. Applicants tend to apply to only a few (or one) college in the fall, so disappointing news has less of a chance to be buoyed by good news.

However, there is still a feeling of a "second chance" in the upcoming spring semester. The high school senior still has time to apply to plenty of schools, perhaps adjusting expectations more realistically this time. He may be able to take standardized tests once more to improve his credentials for regular decision.

Spring is different. Your teen will be able to see all the results of his or her efforts. Disappointments are counterbalanced by gratifying results. Your family will also be receiving news about how much it is going to cost, which may be a key factor in determining the final college choice.

The college process is finally ending. Your kid has laid down his or her hand now, exhausted all senior year options. This sense of finality offers a relief. Your teen has likely sent in enough applications so *something* will work out. If, God forbid, none of the options is sufficiently appealing, *nothing is irrevocable.* Many undergraduates end up transferring for a variety of reasons (not predictable now). Most will ultimately find a fulfilling college experience.

But what if it's "not quite over" by April Fool's Day? I will address three typical "uncertain" situations, with excellent perspective from *Admission Matters: What Students and Parents Need to Know about Getting into College,* by Sally S. Springer, Jon Reider, and Marion R. Franck.[1]

1. Your student has been wait-listed at the first-choice college. *What does that mean?* The authors explain: "Being placed on a wait list means that your file will be considered again if the college has fewer acceptances than it anticipated when mailing out offers of admission. Because no college gets a yes from every admitted student, they will accept more than they can accommodate. On the basis of past experience, they calculate an estimated yield from their offers. Then they wait until after the May 1 deadline to see how many students send in their deposits."[2]

What to do? The authors advise: "A letter notifying you that you have been placed on the wait list includes a postcard asking whether you wish to stay on the wait list. if the wait list college is still an appealing option, you may wish to respond positively knowing your chance of moving from the waitlist is *low...*

"You should also inquire about a college's policy regarding financial aid for students admitted from the wait list...Make sure you send a deposit to one of the colleges where you have been accepted outright by the May 1 deadline."[3]

A college wait list is not like airline passengers flying standby, so it is impossible to know where your "place in line" is. Remember, an admissions committee's goal is to "create a class" that is diverse and well balanced. "So as openings occur, a college may examine the whole freshman class, along with geographic, gender, racial and many other dimensions and fill any perceived gaps."[4]

If the college is still your child's first choice, advise your teen to express his or her interest to her guidance counselor and communicate it directly with admissions. But make sure that a *deposit is sent in by May 1 to a school your student would very much like to attend which has* <u>*outright admitted him or her*</u>. Your teen must de-invest emotionally in the wait list school, and focus on the most likely outcome.

2. The merit scholarship and/or financial aid package offered by your student's first-choice school is not what your family expected. The authors advise: "Once you have all your acceptance and financial aid offers, you may also want to make your top-choice school aware of any offer that is significantly large than the one it sent you if the difference in the aid packages may affect your final choice. Also make its admissions staff aware of any changes in your financial situation that might increase your eligibility for aid. Courteously requesting a financial aid review...is both appropriate and smart. Be prepared, of course, for a negative answer."[5]

Merit- and need-based aid cannot be directly compared. A school offering need-based aid cannot be expected to adjust its package to offset a merit award at another school. However, many families who don't qualify for need-based aid may realistically need merit awards to afford a private college. A school's merit generosity may be the ultimate determining factor for some families' college choice.

3. Your young adult does not have a clear first choice. This may be especially true if admission has been denied at the original first-choice school. Now your teen must decide between two or three schools that might not have been considered "as seriously" before (or perhaps not even visited).

Fortunately, most colleges host special visit days for accepted students before May 1. Even if your teen has visited the campus before, this is a great opportunity to see what the college is really like. Your teen will be courted, without the pressure of wondering, "Could I get in here?" Accepted students attend classes, stay overnight in a dorm, and attend sporting or performing arts events.

These events will help your teen decide, and offer the opportunity to celebrate the wonderful choices your teen has earned through hard work in high school. A rite of passage. *Enjoy!* The final decision will involve many factors, which will be unique for every student and family.

39. Dealing with Rejection

"You can't always get what you want."

-Written by Mick Jagger and Keith Richards,
Performed by the Rolling Stones

April is bittersweet for high school seniors. Most have a college acceptance in hand that makes them pretty happy, but many also have some denials or waitlist situations that leave them feeling confused, angry and disappointed. How can parents, college consultants, and guidance counselors help adolescents with all these intense mixed feelings?

1. To state the obvious, *empathize*. This experience may very well be the first major disappointment of your teen's young life. Unlike an adult, an adolescent does not have many data points to fall back on, in which he or she survived disappointments. He or she has not learned resilience, having not yet had opportunities to test the hypothesis that, "This too shall pass."

College denial is similar to social rejection.[1] After your teen wrote so many passionate, vulnerable, self-revealing essays, the admissions committee still said *no*. Most likely, they simply found a grade or test score unsuitable, but to your child, it still feels like a *personal* rejection. It is a decided exclusion from a community that an applicant has visited, feeling that he or she could truly belong and thrive there. It is like getting turned down for a prom date or a plum job, being excluded from the "in" clique, not making the team, or getting blackballed by a fraternity.

That's painful. In fact, recent studies have shown that social rejection affects the part of the brain that is stimulated by physical pain.[2] Except for the first romantic breakup, it is hard to imagine a more intense experience for an adolescent than being denied admission to his or her dream school. Parents feel the pain too. Let's face it, we get our hearts set on certain college acceptances for our children. But let us not be so focused on grieving the loss of our own dreams that we forget about how much "bigger" these experiences can be for our kids.

2. Remember that teens are egocentric. I don't mean that they are "selfish," *per se* (although some clearly are). Teens' brains are still developing, and they find it difficult seeing a situation from another point of view.

The great developmental psychologist Jean Piaget[3] identified a baby's cognitive inability to see a situation from another's vantage point. Known as *theory of mind*, the ability to infer another's perspective—emotional, intellectual, or visual—improves with age. Studies of infants, toddlers and children have documented gradual improvement in this spatially-related skill.[4]

Iroise Dumontheil at University College London, UK,[5] has recently identified the first behavioral evidence showing that theory of mind is still improving even through teenage years. Her brain scan research suggests that a teenage minds toils harder when inferring the outlook of others, compared with adults. In addition, a brain region implicated in theory of mind, the medial prefrontal cortex, continues to develop through adolescence.[6]

This explains why teenagers may seem calloused to the views of others. But it also sheds light on why adolescents seem to interpret even objective external events so *personally.* Furthermore, consider the "self-esteem" parenting trends and documented increases in teen narcissism in recent deacades.[7] Social scientists Jean Twenge and W. Keith Campbell, authors of *The Narcissim Epidemic: Living in the Age of Entitlement*[8], have studied personality inventories over the years. Their stark conclusion: "American college students score progressively higher on narcissism between the early 1980s and 2006."[9]

So if your son or daughter was denied acceptance at the dream school, for demographic or institutional reasons having nothing to do with him or her, it is hard to convince your teen that it is *"not about you."* Nevertheless, try to describe the factors that go into an admission decision, to mitigate, as much as possible, the "magical thinking"[10] that blurs reality for so many teens. It is helpful to model reality-based interpretations of disappointing life events, for this is not the last one your child will experience.

3. Help your teen accept reality. Consider, and share with your son or daughter, the many reality-based possibilities for the rejection that are beyond an applicant's control.

Demographics are simply a hand we are dealt. It is no one's fault that the baby boomers had kids and created a population explosion; our society has progressively raised expectations that more young people will go to college, and technology has made it possible for applicants to apply to more schools. It is simply a fact of life that your teen is operating in a crowded, competitive landscape as he or she seeks entry to college, and it will be the same for graduate school and the workforce for this generation.

Institutitonal needs are also a fact of life, driven by economic, government, and organizational forces beyond an applicant's control. Perhaps the match between what your teen had to offer and the dream school's specific institutional needs was less than perfect. If your student brought "only" academic merit to the table, he or she may have been at a disadvantage versus other applicants with the good fortune of being able to offer the dream school the perfect ingredients to meet its enrollment needs.

For example, admission advantages may accrue to high-performing athletes in Division I "money" sports; early decision applicants who offer guaranteed yield; underrepresented minorities; and legacies or "development admits."[11] Schools have specific enrollment needs, such as balancing the gender, regional or international representation of the incoming class. Some up-and-coming schools are intent upon raising freshman "stats" to improve their rankings. Colleges are businesses, and every admissions department is trying to "create a class"[12] to meet its institutional goals. Some goals are explicitly stated; others may be inside directives that could not be known by applicants.

A parent should be careful not to explain these realities in a "sour grapes" way, or it will defeat the purpose. A parent can help a young person understand that all of us are born in a certain place and time under specific conditions, which bestows advantages and disadvantages. Our lives are an intricate dance of effort and fate. Having no obstacles is not realistic, nor desirable.

Throughout our kids' lifetime and most of our own, we Americans have generally been blessed with a strong economy, relative affluence, and peace. Our kids have only recently begun to encounter the impact of a recessionary economy. Perhaps in our own complacency, we have been deceived into believing that our children need a "perfect" environment in order to survive and thrive. Greg Esterbrook challenges this idea in *The Progress Paradox: How Life Gets Betters While People Feel Worse.*[13]

As our *Greatest Generation*[14] parents or grandparents will be glad to share *(unsolicited!)*, it is adversity that builds inner strength, determination, grit, and character. We human beings may need adversity just as muscles need resistance to build strength and tone. When we explain life's harsh realities to our children, we are wise to reflect that kind of positive philosophy. They take their cues from us.

4. Help your teen find the silver lining. Your adolescent may be so overwhelmed about the loss of the dream school that he or she may not notice other college choices that are actually quite good. Perhaps your kid was so in love with one option that he or she became rigidly convinced that this was the only option that could bring happiness. You can help your student break free of that all-or-nothing thinking by gently refuting the cognitive distortions.[15]

Helen Keller once said, "When one door of happiness closes, another opens; but often we look so long at the closed door that we do not see the one which has been opened for us."[16] The first deaf-blind individual in history to earn a bachelor of arts degree was propelled by positive, pragmatic thinking, and we can inspire our teens by modeling that kind of perspective as well.

5. Help your teen make contingency plans if necessary. If your teen truly has no appealing choices, help create a "Plan B," such as applying to schools which have no closing application dates or considering the possibility of a future transfer (while giving the school a chance). Finding creative solutions to disappointing events is a key ingredient in resilient living, and your teen might as well learn how to do that as early as possible.

40. Decision-Making 101

Perhaps the truth depends on a walk around the lake.

–Wallace Stevens,
American modernist poet

It has been a tough month for high school seniors. After many months of waiting, the ball was finally in their court. Time for them to take an action, for which many were unprepared: *decide* where to go to college. The decision was particularly complicated for students who were wait-listed at their first-choice school, requiring them to commit to another school before May 1. It was also difficult for those who were offered admission but not sufficient funds (need or merit) to attend their dream school. Or for those who were not truly pleased with their choices, but had to decide, perhaps considering the possibility of future transfer.

As a college consultant, I have been privy to the decision-making process of many adolescents at this pivotal juncture in their young lives. I have observed anguish in young adults who truly grasp the gravity of the decision they are making. I have been impressed with the courage of teens willing to take the leap of a huge geographical move. I have admired the youthful idealism that leads students to defer college for a gap year of community service, actualizing their desire to "change the world."

I never feel sorry for young people because they have to make decisions, even tough ones. Making decisions is a cornerstone of growing up. I have a framed quote by JK Rowling in my office: *"It is our choices that show what we truly are, far more than our abilities."* This "last step" in the college process is indeed the most important, where the rubber meets the road.

Our choices are a Rorschach, an inkblot test onto which we project our goals, passions, and ideals, even our rebellions. College choice is the quintessential ipsative exercise for teens, a forced-choice situation where they must *commit*.

That's why the May first deadline is so ominous. It is a young adult's public, tangible declaration of who he or she is. This is one of the first crossroads in life where such a declaration is so dramatically required. Students will face such crossroads many times again in their lives. Big decisions are always challenging, but each successive decision gets somewhat easier because they will have a foundation of experience and the themes will feel more familiar.

What advice do I give my students?

When I studied marketing at Wharton, I was fascinated with decision-making models that clarified how consumers choose products. I remember formulas that incorporate all the attributes a consumer believes a product has, modified by how important the attribute is to that consumer. The dynamics inherent in those formulas apply to all decisions, even choosing one's college.

Let's say a college has a winning football team. So it rates high on the sports attribute. But maybe you couldn't care less about sports. No matter how great the football team is, that is not a compelling reason for **you** to enroll there. It is not enough to identify a college's strengths; you must isolate the factors you consider *crucial to **your** individual college experience*. Choosing a college is more like a marriage than winning a prize. When forced to choose, *the student clarifies his or her priorities* in graphic relief.

Choosing a college, like any decision, involves both thinking and feeling. In the language of Myers-Briggs: "Those who prefer *thinking* tend to decide things from a more detached standpoint, measuring the decision by what seems reasonable, logical, causal, consistent, and matching a given set of rules. Those who prefer *feeling* tend to come to decisions by associating or empathizing with the situation, looking at it 'from the inside' and weighing the situation to achieve, on balance, the greatest harmony, consensus, and fit."[1]

A young person who prefers thinking-based decisions may need help recognizing that *feelings are data too*. I may ask that student, "If you chose College A, abandoning College B, how would you *feel* tomorrow morning?" A student who prefers feeling-based choices may need help considering all the *factual aspects*: "I know you like the *feeling* that College A is in Boston, but does it offer programs to fit your interests?"

After guiding so many adolescents through the adventure of choosing a college, the psychologist in me has become intrigued with the emerging field of the neuroscientific basis of decision making. An excellent primer on the subject is *How We Decide* by Jonah Lehrer.[2] Blogger Eric Nehrlich's review vividly captures this book's wisdom and relevance to young people's decisions about college. Nehrlich summarizes:

"The rational conscious mind is limited in power...Its strengths are that it can logically process new situations, override our knee-jerk impulses that may not be appropriate to the situation, and come up with responses that have not been tried before. Also, decisions made using the rational path are easy to explain, as they are based in logic. Its weaknesses are that it is slow and has limited capacity and therefore works best on well-defined problems with only a few dimensions to consider.

"The unconscious brain is in many ways the opposite of the rational brain. It is a parallel processor with enormous capacity that can optimize decisions among many conflicting dimensions...complex multivariable problems cannot be answered by pure reason...In fact, if we try to attack such problems with the rational brain, we make poorer choices because we seize on variables that are easy to explain rationally rather than considering all of the possible benefits...

"Lehrer suggests that the best strategy when confronting a complex decision with many variables is to study it carefully to load all of the information into our unconscious brain, and then go do something else (take a walk, go for a drive) while the unconscious brain processes that information. This idea is reflected in the standard trope that the best ideas come in the shower."[3]

So after you have guided your adolescent in viewing the decision in all tangible ways, step back. Suggest that he or she chill out and go out for a walk.

41. First Day of May

No trumpets sound when the important decisions of our life are made. Destiny is made known silently.

–Agnes de Mille,
American dancer and choreographer

"First day of May, things are beginning…our side is winning…hip, hip, hooray!"[1] James Taylor's exuberant love song celebrates the universal rite of spring on my iPod car radio, the joy of new life and hope that accompanies the sweet pastel blossoms, the welcome warm weather, and fresh natural fragrances of the first day of May.

Only I hear the music, but all over the country decisions this week, decisions are quietly being made. As a college counselor who experiences it every year, I welcome May first as the closing of one book and the opening of another. The stressful college process is finally ending. It has been quite a fiery crucible, producing uncertainty and suspense, occasionally disappointment, but ultimately yielding self-discovery, the opportunity to learn through making choices, and a new direction for a young adult's life.

May first is the universal date when enrollment deposits are due, when the time for struggle, acceptance, and decision has finally run out. *Game Over!*

There are still many students on waiting lists, a ubiquitous phenomenon in recent years. Their game has gone into overtime.

These students face the challenge of choosing a school to which to send an enrollment deposit, a school they would really love to attend, not just a lame "second choice" to the school at which they are wait-listed. They know that waiting lists are a long shot.

It is hard for adolescents to go through this white-knuckle ride. There is always that remote hope that they will move off the waiting list, and it is difficult to embrace the May first enrollment commitment that they have no choice but to make. Resolution should appear mid to late May, after colleges have all enrollment information. By late June, many schools will close out their waiting lists, and the game is *really* over.

Now that you know where your young adult is going to college, there is so much to do—a whole new set of wild emotions to process. As JT's splendid song says, *"Things are beginning!"*[2] There is a complicated journey ahead, but before embarking, this is a great occasion to pause and say, *"Congratulations!"*

I am so proud of the seniors I have guided this year, in some small way, to discover themselves and create a future college experience in which they will thrive. Among them is my talented niece, bound for Bucknell this fall. I'm beginning to like blue and orange.

Hip, hip, hooray![3]

42. "Senioritis" And What to Do about It

The most precious gift we can offer anyone is our attention.

—Thich Nhat Hanh,
Buddhist monk, teacher, author, poet, and peace activist

Penney Riegelman was head of Newark Academy for most of my son's years there. Wise and witty, she warned parents of what to expect when *"senioritis"* would eventually hit our own students. During senior year fall, we were so worked up about college applications, we never expected that the dreaded senioritis malady would ever really come.

"One day your kid will be so agreeable, responsible, and grown up, making you feel bittersweet about the eventual parting," Penney would say. "The next day he will be so obnoxious you can't wait for him to leave!"

A nod to the schizophrenic spring to come. A recollection of long ago, when our children courageously sought the adventure of the preschool playground, then scurried back to cling to Mom's hand just when she was about to drive away. Those transitional periods as a growing child encounters each new situation, with its confusion, frustration, and mixed feelings, was once described by psychologist Jean Piaget as *"disequilibrium."* [1]

"We invented senior projects to combat senioritis," Penney explained. "After the AP tests, seniors see no reason to be on campus. *And we don't want them there!* We don't want juniors catching their contagious *ennui*. They are feeling their new powers, as almost-grads, and want to flex their muscles. So we give them an independent project to conduct off campus. They return before commencement to present results to their peers."

The Launching Years: Strategies for Parenting from Senior Year to College Life[2] describes the "fall flurry" of applications, followed by "winter limbo and spring flings." Authors L. Kastner and J. Wyatt explain why *senioritis* happens now: "Although twinges of senioritis surface sporadically over an extended period, it's typically at its worst once applications are finished...seniors are freed up to express directly other feelings related to launching that have been pushed aside."[3] They identify three hallmarks:

"**1. An Academic Slump.** Every college counselor and admissions representative warns seniors to keep up their grades during winter and spring, but no matter how many times they hear, 'Your grades still count,' seniors feel *battle fatigue* for school."[4]

"**2. 'Blahs' to Everything.**...A blanket of weariness and ambivalence can descend on their world. Sick of everything and everyone, many disengage...friends are a little annoying... The old sameness isn't there because they feel *themselves* changing... the disconnect among some peers is often followed by bonding madly with them around graduation."[5]

"**3. Power Surges.** Think back on the defiance of the 'terrible twos' and the bridling behaviors of middle school. Winter of senior year signals another onset of a push for autonomy. Just as a two year old... informs her parents, 'You're not the boss of me,' eighteen-year-olds spar with their parents during transition to adulthood, as if to say, 'I don't want to answer to you anymore.'... Well-adjusted adolescents survive periodic risk-taking, but this is also a time for parents to keep a watchful eye."[6]

The authors wisely observe that parents, and in fact, **the whole family, can contract senioritis.** "Parents can no longer escape the stressful realization that it's the beginning of the end of their child-rearing years. Many are dealing with their own midlife issues (job, health, loss of youth) and elderly parents."[7] We tend to forget the impact on the high school senior's *siblings*. Although siblings "balance a love-hate relationship with older brothers and sisters, [they] may panic at the prospect of being alone at home."[8]

This book offers insightful observations such as, "The compulsion is for parents to work overtime to put finishing touches on their children before leaving home."[9] The authors also proffer tactical advice given the level of the high school senior's maturity and sense of responsibility.

The most essential tool for surviving senioritis, I feel, is an *awareness* that this is a natural, transitional process. *Flexibility* will not make it painless, but will ease the struggle somewhat.

Remember that after this roller-coaster ride is over, you still want to salvage a relationship with your son or daughter for the future. This may mean biting your tongue, taking the high ground, and above all, *listening with full attention and love*. Ultimately, you will forge a new relationship with this emerging young adult who is sometimes hard to recognize, especially senior year.

When my son graduated, Penney had moved on to a new position, but she returned for commencement. After the ceremony, Eric made rounds with teachers and peers, touching base with me only to hand me a plastic cup after finishing his Coke. I mentioned this incident to Penney, bemoaning the fact that this "grown-up grad" was still handing me his trash, just like back in preschool.

Penney smiled wryly and said, "And as long as you keep accepting it, he'll keep giving it to you." There is always more to learn in the ever-evolving relationship between parents and their growing children.

43. No Guts, No Glory

So be there to listen, and be there to talk, and learn to let go when
it's her time to walk...

–Written by P. Vassar, J. Outlaw, and T. Nichols,
Performed by Phil Vassar, American singer-songwriter

"Now, will the Class of 2010 please rise."

All over the USA this month, parents, grandparents, aunts and uncles, siblings, friends, teachers, guidance counselors, and college consultants heard those pivotal words. Despite humidity, worry about rain and camera battery longevity, the reality of the moment has broken through everywhere with elegant matter-of-factness.

Eighteen years ago, 4.1 million babies were born in the USA, slightly less than the millennials' birth peak in 1990. *What a year, 1992...*[1]

Disney's *Aladdin*, the top-grossing film, was almost as popular with my two-year-old son as Thomas the Tank Engine and his Brio® trains. Bill Clinton was elected forty-second President of the United States. The Summer Olympic Games were held in Barcelona, Spain. The world had just witnessed the dissolution of the Soviet Union. And a talented country singer, Suzy Bogguss, gave the world a unique gift with the chart-topping crossover ballad about parent-child rite of passage: "Letting Go."[2]

In 1992, I left my marketing position with Nabisco, enrolling in graduate psychology at Columbia University, to study career counseling and spend more time with my little boy. That was the year I lost my mother. And my twin sister had her first child.

It became my sister's custom to wear a big old T-shirt of her husband's to the hospital when giving birth to each of her daughters. The T-shirt read: ***"No guts, no glory."***

Fast forward eighteen years. It's taken a lot of guts to get here. Sleepless nights interrupted by infant cries; tearful preschool good-byes; mind-numbing, noisy birthday parties; spectating on pins and needles at soccer games, ballet recitals, spelling bees, auditions, and theater productions; quelling the drama of sibling disputes; feeling the vicarious wounds of any rejection or disappointment; intense midnight debates on the meaning of life; voracious shopping for prom shoes; resisting the proverbial temptation to backseat drive; surviving those wild teenage mood swings; arguing about the college essay; sleepless nights wondering how to pay for her dream school…

No, parenthood is *not for wimps*. You've had the guts so far, and you'll need them forever. But tonight, it's time for a little glory.

Cornwall Central High School in New York's Hudson Valley welcomes a commencement speaker who knows a little about guts and glory: General David Petraeus, head of US Central Command and Cornwall's most famous alumnus.

This week the four-star general was nominated by President Obama as the new commander of U.S. forces in Afghanistan, perhaps his most daunting challenge to date. Yet, this man of his roots is still making time for the high school seniors at his alma mater. This evening, I am honored and thrilled to be audience to his keynote address, and I listen thoughtfully to the wisdom the great hero offers.

The general bases his inspirational speech on a quote from the Nobel prize-winning writer Anatole France: *"To accomplish great things, we must not only act, but also dream; not only plan, but also believe."* He dramatizes this quotation in graphic relief with moving anecdotes from his own incredible career and courageous life.

Forty years ago, David "Peaches" Petraeus, son of Miriam (neé Howell), a librarian, and Sextus Petraeus, a sea captain, stood with his own graduating class from this close-knit, modest Hudson Valley community, anticipating the future's possibilities. Now, some 280 new high school graduates are doing the same, and my niece, Laura, is among them.

Maneuvering behind the sea of chairs, trying to get the best camera angle, I begin reminiscing about my niece's growing up, smiling as I anticipate her undoubtedly bright future. I recall a few words from "She's on Her Way,"[3] Phil Vassar's touching song about girls growing up: *"So be there to listen, and be there to talk, and learn to let go when it's her time to walk..."*

My niece accepts her diploma, sixth in her class, with many honors. I am a proud aunt.

Glory over. Now back to the guts.

VI. Off to College

44. The College Transition "Bible"

Veni, Vidi, Vici.

–Julius Caesar,
Roman general, emperor, and statesman

How to get ready for the *Big Move?*

Except for that leftover cake in the fridge, high school graduation is over. Of course, he's not ready to think about becoming a college freshman *just yet.* He's thinking about parties, summer jobs, and beach trips with friends, and what (in his mind) will be an endless summer.

But *you're* thinking about college. You have mixed feelings about him going, but you've got to plan the big move. My husband says that mothers plan a kid's move to college the same way women plan weddings: like generals staging a military campaign.

So what is your strategy of attack?

Like most huge tasks, I start with organization. For my son's move, I assembled a binder with all key pieces of information in it, made a copy for my son and for me. Some of this project we did in tandem, some fell to me. I didn't mind, since I knew that chapter of our relationship would so quickly pass. The college transition "bible" as I began to call it, had sections that I'll share with you:

Dorm checklist: Download a list from your school's Web site, with instructions about what or what not to bring. Take note of rules about *microwaves* (colleges often specify a micro fridge combo model you can buy or rent), *extension cords* (power surge protectors preferred), and *light bulbs* (halogen bulbs are forbidden). Find out if you are allowed to "loft" beds and buy a futon for underneath.

Confirm what furniture and interiors are included before purchasing anything. Check with the roommate before buying a TV, speakers, computer printer, air filter, large fan, and other major electronics. *A great excuse for roommates touching base before they arrive!*

Before buying a laptop, check with the school (some colleges supply laptops, most offer discounts); consider small electronics insurance as a homeowner's rider; and buy a laptop lock (yes, they get stolen at the nicest colleges). For cell phones, consider insurance; make sure the phone offers a seamless shift between voice, text, and e-mail (easier to reach your kid); consider camera and media features to minimize the need for buying additional electronics. Many dorm rooms do not have landline phones.

Bed Bath & Beyond, Staples, JC Penney, Wal-Mart, Target, Container Store, and Pottery Barn are the obvious shopping resources. Most of them offer helpful online, printable dorm checklists that you can slip into the binder.

Travel information: Essential if your student has to fly to college. Or for accommodations reservations on the way or during move-in.

US mail, package shipping, and summer storage addresses: If your kid is going far away, it may make sense to buy dorm gear online and have it shipped directly to college, if they offer a summer storage address. Some national store chains offer an option for buying dorm gear in advance and picking it up at the store location near your college during move-in.

Copies of important documents: Completed insurance, medical, and proof of immunization forms. Copy of insurance card, meds prescriptions, glasses prescriptions (so they can get a new pair if–*when* they lose them), passport numbers if any international travel is involved during the first year.

Maps of campus and local area: Download campus maps from the college Web site and Google area maps. Mark off locations of grocery, pharmacy, office supply, big box stores, malls, and restaurants. GPS is great, but having a few maps gives you the lay of the land.

Orientation schedule: Download from the college Web site so you don't have to keep going to your laptop to find out what is happening when.

Emergency phone numbers: You can never have too many copies, no matter how often your kid says the numbers are in the cell phone (they *lose* cell phones).

It's *"mise en place"* (all ingredients in place) all over again, just like at the beginning of your student's high school career.

Iea Iacta Est! *("The Die Is Cast")*

–Julius Caesar,
Roman general, emperor, and statesman

45. College Orientation Rites

Every new beginning comes from some other beginning's end.

–Seneca the Younger,
Roman Stoic philosopher, statesman, and writer

Most freshmen will experience an avalanche of initiatory rites in the next few weeks. Some already had their orientation back in June. But for many, this is the first time they will set foot on campus since their first tour over a year ago. The edge of a great beginning. Here's what to expect:

Many colleges offer optional outdoor pre-orientation programs to help small groups of freshmen bond through recreation, fitness, or adventure trips before the official orientation week begins. College students often say that they find some of their best, long-lasting friendships that first week on an outdoor pre-orientation trip. Activities can include camping, hiking, mountain biking, rafting, kayaking, water skiing, sailing, challenge courses—the list goes on. Don't worry, no skydiving. They'll do that on their own, *just to torture you!*

Some colleges also offer optional community service pre-orientation programs. These programs are great for freshmen who may not be "into" the outdoors, who would rather serve their college's surrounding community, while also getting acquainted with each other.

Typically, dorm move-in immediately follows pre-orientation (some schools allow freshmen to move in prior to pre-orientation trips).

Formal programs for students and parents begin shortly thereafter, with social activities to help freshmen get acquainted during the evenings. Having met my husband of thirty years at a dorm party the first week of school, I am a big believer that even the shyest student should make an effort to reach out at these events.

You can expect formal orientation schedules to include receptions, discussion panels, campus tours, president's welcome events, academic department fairs, activity fairs, and religious services. Parents are then politely asked to "depart" (*such an understatement*). After the "'rents" are gone, orientation becomes more focused, with academic advising, placement exams, and class enrollment.

Make good use of time when your teen is away on a pre-orientation trip or social activity during orientation. Get the lay of the land, so you can suggest close-by grocery stores, pharmacies, hair salons, office supply stores, UPS stores, and eateries. Check out where shuttles and buses stop; locate nearby subway or light rail stations.

If you haven't bought all the dorm room items yet, find a Staples, Bed Bath & Beyond, Target, Wal-Mart, JC Penney, or Container Store in the area. If it's too stressful to schlep multiple loads, you can rent also a cargo van for under $20 a day with Budget or U-Haul. Don't forget the Advil. Your muscles will ache at the end of the day. You will sleep well.

If this is your first child going to college, keeping busy will have another benefit too…and *you know what it is.*

The moment is coming. It will be different for everyone. Hopefully, you have talked about the separation now and again over the summer, so there has been some natural preparation. My advice is, be genuine, but don't overdo it. Your goal is to help your child process this transition and feel good about the new world he or she is entering, *not* let it all hang out.

46. The Hero's Journey

There's a way, and I know: I have to go away.

—Written and performed by Cat Stevens,
British singer-songwriter, philanthropist, now Yusef Islam

My sister, Karen, and her daughter, Laura, just returned from the beauty salon. They did the school spirit pedicure, with Bucknell's blue and orange colors on alternating toenails, and the signature *B* on the big toes. Their outing reflected not only my niece's enthusiasm for her new freshman adventure, but a nod to the mother-daughter bond, in no way over but *evolving* into an adult relationship.

One more day of packing the car with Bed Bath & Beyond dorm gear for the drive to Pennsylvania. Meanwhile, my son, Eric, and I are preparing to drive his red and white Mini Cooper to Atlanta to begin his junior year at Emory. We are far more casual (I haven't painted my toenails blue and gold), but our adult relationship continues to evolve as well.

There is much written about the rite of passage of going away to college, both for the young adult leaving and the family staying behind. Some may believe that too much is made of it in our culture. However, I feel that this undertaking captures the modern imagination because it has all the psychological trappings of the start of the archetypal hero's great odyssey.

Mythologist Joseph Campbell explains the monomyth of the hero's journey in his classic book, *Hero with a Thousand Faces*: "A hero ventures forth from the world of common day into a region of supernatural wonder: fabulous forces are there encountered and a decisive victory is won: the hero comes back from this mysterious adventure with the power to bestow boons on his fellow man."[1]

George Lucas' *Star Wars*[2] emphasizes the part of the archetypal myth in which the hero must "kill his father" to grow up and grasp his destiny.[3] In the twenty-first-century reincarnation of the myth, conflict between parent and teen culminates in the adolescent's ultimate bid for autonomy, figuratively "killing" his parents by going to college.

Judith Viorst writes about separation from our parents as essential to adult growth and development in her psychoanalytic masterpiece, *Necessary Losses: The Loves, Illusions, Dependencies, and Impossible Expectations That All of Us Have to Give Up in Order to Grow.*[4]

Yusef Islam, formerly Cat Stevens, summed it up in his classic song, "Father and Son" from *Tea for the Tillerman*: "There's a way, and I know: I have to go away."[5]

47. Letting Go

She's had eighteen years to get ready for this day. She should be past the tears, she cries some anyway...It's never easy, letting go.

—Written by D. Crider and M. Rollins,
Performed by Suzy Bogguss, American singer-songwriter

Launching a college student is such an individual experience. Whether you work or have other children, everybody deals with it a little differently. It is probably fair to say, however, that the experience is filled with mixed feelings, and *is certainly not easy.*

We baby boomers, the intensity generation, have hurled our hearts and souls into every chapter of our lives. As the first generation to choose when to become parents, we naturally became *passionate parents*, elevating parenting to the apex of Maslow's Hierarchy, playing Mozart to make our children "smarter" in utero. Some of us became soccer moms, then some became helicopter parents, occasionally taking our passion to an unhealthy extreme that deterred, rather than advanced, our children's autonomy and self-esteem.[1]

When one's child—especially the "only" or last one—leaves for college, what does a parent do *with all that passion?*

As my son graduated high school and left for Emory University, my husband said, "It must be difficult getting 'fired' from your 'job' after eighteen years." He was right. If you do your job as a parent well, your son or daughter will probably become independent and effective, so the reward is being fired even more quickly! You're always connected, but now your "kid" is a grown-up who can fend for him or herself. That was the goal, after all, wasn't it?

When I was first struggling with this paradox, one parent quipped, *"Get a life!"* Another philosophized, *"Find a new source of meaning, and try not to get too fat."* My own take is that parenting a child at home for eighteen years is so all-absorbing and purposeful, that one cannot simply turn off a switch and disengage.

A parent of a college freshman cannot expect to "get a life" overnight. Such an oversimplification glosses over the genuine grief-loss components and midlife transition issues encountered when one's kids leave home. Like every stage in life, I believe this new chapter must be navigated with patience, reflection, and creativity, and it can offer new sources of meaning and personal legacy.

My son's first year at Emory brought an avalanche of new adventures—for both of us. I shuddered when he called me from a landing strip in Georgia, gleefully reporting that he had just taken his first sky dive. *Thank God he didn't tell me before he stepped out of the plane!* Not to be outdone, a few months later I tried hang gliding from a 2,700-foot cliff with one of my best friends in Rio de Janeiro.

During that year, I launched Position U 4 College, built a new kitchen, attended "Charting Your Course" at Harvard, [2] swam with dolphins and manatees, held a tiger cub, painted acrylic landscapes, lost a few pounds and a lot of money in the stock market, and supported a dear friend tragically diagnosed with ALS, Lou Gehrig's disease. I missed my son, watched him grow from afar, and became even prouder of my son.

After the emotional roller-coaster experience of launching a college freshman, a new relationship begins to unfold, between parents and a young, however provisional, adult. One of the best kept secrets is that it is far more pleasant than the stormy parent-teen relationship. Other goals begin to emerge for parents too, in their work, relationships, and as human beings. It is a process that takes time, mixing joy and loss with eventual new self-discovery.

How to get through it?

Music helps. For me, every life experience needs a soundtrack. Let me suggest a few special songs that may reveal my age, nostalgic, cathartic, or wise, to help you navigate these new ambivalent waters. My favorite is Suzy Bogguss' classic, "Letting Go."[3]

There's a song out there for every emotion: Cat Stevens' "Father and Son,"[4] Phil Vassar's "She's on Her Way,"[5] Lee Ann Womack's "I Hope You Dance,"[6] John Mellencamp's "Your Life Is Now,"[7] and "For Good," performed by Idina Menzel and Kristin Chenoweth in the Broadway hit musical *Wicked*.[8] And don't forget Dixie Chicks' "Wide Open Spaces."[9]

Books help. To help parents manage relationships with their college students, I suggest the classic: *Letting Go (5th Edition): A Parent's Guide to Understanding the College Years* by Karen Levin Coburn and Madge Lawrence Treeger;[10] *Don't Tell Me What to Do, Just Send Money: The Essential Parent Guide to the College Years* by Helen E. Johnson and Christine Schelhas-Miller; [11] and *Almost Grown: Launching Your Child from High School to College* by therapist Patricia Pasick.[12]

I can recommend a few books to help your freshman get a good start in college. You may be able to pass them along as gifts, if your freshman is open. One great choice is: *How to Become a Straight-A Student: The Unconventional Strategies Real College Students Use to Score High While Studying Less* by Cal Newport.[13] Harlan Cohen has written two excellent books, *The Naked Roommate: And 107 Other Issues You Might Run into in College*[14] and *The Happiest Kid on Campus: A Parent's Guide to the Very Best College Experience (for You and Your Child)*. [15]

To help parents navigate their own new journey, I can suggest: *Barbara & Susan's Guide to the Empty Nest: Discovering New Purpose, Passion & Your Next Great Adventure* by Barbara Rainey and Susan Yates; [16] *Back on the Career Track: A Guide for Stay-at-Home Moms Who Want to Return to Work* by Carol Fishman Cohen and Vivian Steir Rabin,[17] co-founders of the career re-entry organization iRelaunch;[18] and *Finding Meaning in the Second Half of Life* by Jungian analyst James Hollis.[19]

48. College Move-In: The Aftermath

Making the decision to have a child is momentous. It is to decide forever to have your heart go walking around outside your body.

–Elizabeth Stone,
American author

My shoulders ached, despite the Advils I'd been taking all day. I had just finished move-in for my son's sophomore year at Emory. I finished my Diet Coke, so fitting at *"Coca-Cola University."* It was thankfully unseasonably cool for Atlanta in August, with a refreshing breeze and dappled sunlight smiling through the shade of young peach trees around the stately, columned fraternity house. It felt like September, another new beginning.

We'd done all the things you're not allowed to do in a freshman dorm. We lofted the bed (a Herculean task) and purchased a futon for underneath. I arranged my son's books, desk supplies, Xbox games, lamps, and memorabilia on his desk and shelves, and hung up or folded his clothes. We hooked up the electronics. His room looked better than it would look *for the rest of the year!* We took a BlackBerry photo to e-mail to everyone back home. Eric laughed, "Don't worry, Mom, I'll *de-mom-ify* it after you leave."

I smiled at my son. I was so proud of him. He had changed quite a bit during his first year in college. A year ago, he was a reluctant freshman, trying to grasp the lay of the land of a scary new world, wondering whether he would succeed on this new proving ground. Now, with impressive academic performance, selection of a major, fraternity bro's, and a summer internship under his belt, my son had emerged as a confident young adult. *What a difference a year makes.*

Parents who are launching their first freshman can rest reassured. You *will* survive this first separation. And each year, it will get easier, because your student will be one year closer to autonomous, responsible adulthood. Your children are in good hands: *their own.*

When you leave your freshman and begin that long drive or flight home, there is a feeling of vacancy, a pang that makes your eyes well up. You miss your son or daughter terribly. Freshman year is definitely the toughest. You will probably experience a complex mix of excitement, grief, and anxiety about the unknown of your relationship with your young adult, and his or her ability to thrive at college. If this is your only child, you may feel anxious about your ability to build a new life without a dependent child at the center. If you have other children at home, you may wonder how the family dynamics will now change.

If this is the beginning of your empty nest chapter, it may be a good idea to not go straight home. You and your spouse could go away on a long-deserved getaway. Plan projects, meaningful work, and bucket list adventures to which you can look forward.

Check in with your new college student every few days at first, then once a week, or whatever feels comfortable. Your freshman will probably touch base with you only when it is most convenient—a few words or text messages on the way to class.

Conversations may be abruptly aborted upon arrival at the dining hall, or when another student meets up with yours on the Quad. "Hall bonding" always takes precedence over parental phone calls. Take what you can get. If you don't hear from your kid, that's probably a good sign. Be there when your freshman needs you. Listen.

You are the mother ship, remember! Your young adult is exploring independence in a bigger way than ever before, but it is essential that he or she can touch base with the mother ship whenever necessary.

Send care packages. My favorite is the Popcorn Factory. Plan to visit for family weekend. Be a sounding board, especially if your college student needs to discuss an issue, such as dropping a class early on or an escalating roommate problem. You'll get into a rhythm. Different than before, but it will become more natural as time goes on. This is the beginning of your adult relationship.

49. Helicopter Parents: College and Beyond

The trouble with being a parent is that by the time you are experienced, you are unemployed.

–Anonymous

The Emory University tour for prospective families traversed the beautiful Atlanta campus on a fragrant spring day in 2007, ultimately persuading my son that this was the ideal place for his college experience. When the admissions tour guide led us around Emory's state-of-the-art medical complex, she happened to point out a helipad for emergency transport.

Never able to resist a comic opportunity, I chimed in, *"Is that for the helicopter parents?"* The sophomore tour guide seemed flustered by my unorthodox question, and some nervous parents glared. But the wiser parents flashed knowing smiles—and *all* the teenagers giggled.

At the time, I meant only to poke fun at parents who micromanage their high school students through the college process. I did not yet realize that for many families today, the "helicopter parents" phenomenon continues throughout the college years…and even into the careers of emerging young adults!

A recent article in *US News and World Report,* "10 Reasons Why Parents Should Never Contact College Professors,"[1] confirms that helicoptering can and does continue way beyond dorm dropoff. No wonder freshman orientations include presentations about "letting go" for parents, and schedules designate a specific time when "PARENTS DEPART."

It's not just because faculty and students find hovering parents overbearingly annoying. A recent study by psychologist Neil Montgomery[2] at Keene State College in New Hampshire suggests that students with hyper managing parents tend to be *less open to new ideas and actions*, and may be *more vulnerable, anxious, and self-conscious*, compared to students with more distant parents.

I just finished reading *The iConnected Parent: Staying Close to Your Kids in College (and Beyond) While Letting Them Grow Up* [3] co-authored by Barbara K. Hofer, a professor at Middlebury College in Vermont and journalist Abigail Sullivan Moore. This thought-provoking 2010 book was based on a 2005 study at Middlebury and a 2006 study at the University of Michigan.

The authors expand on the helicopter concept by demonstrating the role technology plays to enable parental micromanaging of students' lives when they no longer live at home. Many parents are in constant contact with their kids at college via cell, text, e-mail, Facebook, and Skype.

The Middlebury and University of Michigan studies indicate that many parents edit their children's papers via e-mail, a behavior that was not feasible during our snail mail past. Some parents intervene in academic decisions such as choosing majors or contacting professors to dispute grades. *Middle school parent-teacher conference redux?*

Technology-enabled "hyper" managing even continues into young people's career search activities. The studies revealed that some moms and dads actually log in with their kids' passwords and fill out job applications, write resumes and cover letters, and even contact employers on behalf of their grown children. *Oy! Where does it end?*

The authors concede that over parenting is passionate parenting taken a little too far. Many baby boomers, having fewer children later in life, view our progeny as so "precious" that we try to protect them from risks in this decade's competitive college process and the depressed job market. Few become *Blackhawks*, a coinage for parents who cross the line from excess zeal to unethical behavior, such as actually writing their kids' papers.

And we *do* want to remain connected to our kids, don't we? It's a tough world out there, and intergenerational connection is a desirable, natural, time-honored source of support through life. Hopefully, however, we can stave off the controlling attitude that could potentially poison relationships with our adult children.

Hofer and Moore suggest that over parenting through constant, overbearing contact hinders college students' personal growth, and robs young adults of the opportunity to make decisions and learn from mistakes. They point out that excessive, controlling communication is not only detrimental to students, but it also exacerbates parents' own anxiety.

The authors recommend *a moderate, balanced approach* that retains connection but empowers our kids to find their own way. I couldn't agree more. Follow your instincts, resist the temptation to fill every vacuum and answer every question, and most importantly, LISTEN to feedback. After all, it's their turn now.

50. Adjusting to College Life: "Friendsickness"

Home is not where you live but where they understand you.

—Christian Morgenstern,
Nineteenth C. German author and poet

Your college freshman will make many new adjustments, from doing laundry to managing a heavy academic load independently. But I'd like to focus on one key adjustment, establishing *new social connections.*

Psychologists E. Brier and S. Paul coined the term "friendsickness" as *"the pressing relational challenge for new college students that is induced by moving away from an established network of friends."*[1] Freshmen miss their families, but they also miss *high school friends!* They miss the comfort of peers who have known them a long time, who "get" them, without their having to struggle to gain acceptance.

Freshmen always have their parents and families for support. However, as researcher J.R. Stenrud[2] has pointed out, friendships, due to their voluntary nature, are more difficult to maintain than are family ties; therefore, they often represent a more *final sense of loss.*

Preoccupation and grief associated with precollege friendships actually prevent freshmen from investing in new relationships, increasing further the risk for "friendsickness" and adjustment difficulties. Text/IMing make it easier to stay in touch, but also distract students from engaging in the "here and now."

Jennifer C. Ishler, assistant professor of Human Development and Family Studies at Penn State, traced the phenomenon of friendsickness through the first year of college through female students' journal writing in her freshman seminar.[3]

Professor Ishler observed: "[Students taking the seminar first semester] missed their friends from home and delayed making new friends at college for fear of betraying the friends they left behind. This sense of loyalty to old friends prohibited the new students from fully committing to their new college life. As a result, they did not start connecting to a new peer group, often felt lonely, and did not connect with the social aspect of their new environment."[4]

Students who took Ishler's seminar during their second semester were clearly in a different place. "[They] wrote in their journals about the new friends they had made in college, how close they had become to these people in just a matter of months, how their new friends had helped them adjust to their new environment, and how they were going to miss their new friends over the summer. Students during the spring semester came to realize that precollege friendships did not exclude the formation of new friendships, but that both could co-exist." [5]

What can parents do to help freshman make smooth transition from grieving old friendships to making new connections at college?

The philosophical answer is, you don't have to do *anything*, just let your child's personal experience unfold naturally. By second semester, your freshman will feel connected at school, while maintaining historical friendships.

If your child needs help connecting, here are some ideas you can suggest:

1. Take a freshman seminar first versus second semester. Many colleges require freshman seminars now, to ensure a first year opportunity to be in a small discussion class that guarantees interaction with faculty and classmates. The seminar is intended to counterbalance the anonymous lecture hall setting of introductory courses. Doing it fall semester ensures your child will have *at least one class* which is an engaging experience *right away*.

2. Join at least one extracurricular activity. It's obvious but essential. Your child can try something new, or enjoy an activity that has brought satisfaction and self-confidence throughout high school. Importantly, it will offer the opportunity to become connected.

3. If a roommate situation is clearly not working out, change it quickly. It's just lousy luck, but it can ruin a kid's first semester in college. If there is an opportunity to change a really bad situation, encourage your child to seize the chance. This is especially critical if the roommate is a substance abuser or if your teen becomes constantly "sexiled."[6]

4. Keep a journal. Ishler found that journal-writing itself helped freshmen process friendsickness. It is a time-honored resource for all human beings, including adolescents, to reflect on their experiences and development. [7]

5. Encourage a "wait-and-see" attitude. Some teens interpret the initial stressors of college, including friendsickness, as a reason for transferring or dropping out. Such a proclamation can cause a parent shock and distress. (Was all that work trying to get your child accepted to "First-Choice U" *in vain?*) Counsel your teen to give it time. Meanwhile, remind your teen that to be in the position to transfer, great grades are required! It's a win-win if your freshman gets impressive grades, and then still wants to stay.

51. When Big Brother or Sister Goes to College

Siblings: the definition that comprises love, strife, competition, and forever friends.

–Byron Pulsifier,
Motivational speaker

Years ago, when the first-born daughter of family friends was leaving for college, I attempted to comfort the more reserved younger daughter, who was trying to prepare emotionally for her beloved sister's departure. The two siblings had a close relationship, and I knew they would miss each other very much.

Trying to find the silver lining, I said, "Now your parents will be able to give you their full attention!" After a few moments of silence, she replied, "Yeah. *That's what I'm afraid of!*"

More recently, when my older niece, Laura, left for college, her middle school sister, Caroline, welcomed the chance to take center stage. Both bright and talented girls, there had always been competition between them. Covering her sibling's high school graduation photo with her hands, Caroline triumphantly proclaimed, *"Sister no more!"*

As a psychology graduate student, I studied family systems, group dynamics, and grief counseling. I learned that whenever someone "exits the stage" of any group, it affects that system's dynamics as everyone scrambles to assume different roles, compensating for the loss of the individual who has left the scene (e.g., going to college, moving out, getting married or divorced, passing away). Who will be the "peacemaker" now that the "peacemaker" has left for college? The troublemaker, the worrier, the life of the party, the angry one, the analyzer, the soother, the communicator, the justice seeker?

My husband and I experienced the requisite painful readjustment when our only son left for college: the classic "empty nest" has received the attention it deserves as a major life transition. However, when a family has multiple children, the domino effect of one child leaving on the remaining siblings has not received as much focus. I can only imagine that the interactive, dynamic effects are profound, warranting discussion, empathy, and support!

Siblings dealing with the loss (*yes, loss!*) of a big brother or sister who departs for college is NOT as easy to find in self-help books as advice about getting your kid into college and surviving freshman year.

I have found only two books with brief chapters devoted to the siblings left behind: *Don't Tell Me What to Do, Just Send Money: The Essential Parent Guide to the College Years* by Helen E. Johnson and Christine Schelhas-Miller[1] and *Almost Grown: Launching Your Child from High School to College* by therapist Patricia Pasick.[2]

Be sensitive to the possible feelings that siblings may be experiencing when this change in family structure takes place. Be there to notice, to ask, and to listen.

52. College Family Weekends: Forever Jung

*In the middle of the road of my life I awoke in the dark wood
where the true way was wholly lost.*

–Dante Alighieri,
Thirteenth C. Italian poet

It was one of those crisp, breezy October Saturdays in the rolling hills of Pennsylvania, with the leaves just beginning to sport a bit of gold and copper under a cloudless cobalt sky. It was Family Weekend at Bucknell University, in the idyllic colonial town of Lewisburg on the west branch of Susquehanna River.

My husband and I joined my sister's family to celebrate our niece's joyful first semester at Bucknell, shamelessly donning blue and orange. My husband was especially thrilled to go to a family weekend with a Saturday football game, of which he felt deprived when my son matriculated to Emory University in fall 2008, famous for its *lack* of a football team and its ubiquitous T-shirt: "Emory Football: Still Undefeated."

We were *wowed* by the University Orchestra under the direction of Christopher Para and the internationally renowned Rooke Chapel Choir and Rooke Chapel Ringers conducted by William Payn. We left wishing to be young again, able to freely partake of such superb intellectual and cultural stimulation on a daily basis.

All over the country, parents are visiting colleges for family weekends, especially their recently launched freshmen. For most families, it is the first face-to-face since dorm move-in. It is a time to reconnect, check in and take a pulse, and hopefully find that the kid is "settling in" just fine. *With fingers crossed not to fall into the trap of sparring in the first ten minutes!*

As a parent, aunt, college consultant, and lifelong psychology aficionado, I was most fascinated by a presentation by Bucknell's Psychological Services interim director, Dr. Thomas Balistrieri, PhD, known to my niece simply as "Dr. Tom." I expected the typical *"no helicopters"* speech, but to my surprise, Dr. Tom introduced a new and intriguing concept I had never heard before: **LIMINALITY.**

Liminality (from the Latin word *līmen*, meaning "a threshold") is a psychological, neurological, or metaphysical subjective state, conscious or unconscious, of being on the "threshold" of or between two different existential planes. Liminality is a term often used in anthropology, when discussing rites of passage.[1]

Folklorist Arnold van Gennep identified three phases of *rites of passage:* separation, transition and finally re-incorporation.[2] Anthropologist Victor Turner described the transitional, or *liminal*, phase as "the period between states, during which one has left one place or state but hasn't yet entered or joined the next."[3]

Carl Jung's depth psychology refers to a liminal phase in *individuation,* the process by which a person becomes his or her "true self."[4] Jungian analyst Bani Shorter wrote: "Individuation can be seen as a 'movement through liminal space and time, from disorientation to integration...What takes place in the dark phase of liminality is a process of breaking down...in the interest of 'making whole' one's meaning, purpose and sense of relatedness once more."[5]

There are many transitional, or liminal, periods in each of our lives. One of the most vivid examples is the passage from adolescent to young adult, marked by the physical separation from family of origin brought about by moving to college; initial disorientation and being in a state of flux; and eventually integrating new perspectives as an independent, whole young adult.

As Dr. Tom spoke, I couldn't help but notice the irony that while college students are experiencing a period of liminality, so too are their parents. It would be so reassuring if parents were unchanging "Rocks of Gibraltar" while their college students were in such a shifting state, but generally *they are not.*

Parents too are entering a liminal period in their lives, doubling the sense of disorientation during the college years. I contemplated all the experiences parents of college students often encounter: empty nesting, home downsizing or relocation, midlife crisis, menopause, eldercare, divorce, remarriage, career relaunch, retirement. A kid going off to college is really a new chapter for everybody in the family.

Dr. Tom explained that it is imperative during a liminal phase in one's life to find a sacred, safe place for grounding. Professors, counselors, and resident assistants who mentor in a boundaried, responsible way can give centered guidance to young adults in a stage of searching, flux, and self-discovery.

In her Sunday sermon at the Rooke Chapel, Bucknell's chaplain, the radiant Reverend Thomasina Yuille, also talked about freshmen navigating this disorienting new chapter. She wisely reminded us that *virtue* offers the anchor in a period of flux, both in the supportive college community a student has chosen and in the student's own character.

Families should seek out potential colleges that clearly offer such guidance and support. Rather than focusing on academic ranking, identify colleges that guide the student's transformational process from teen to adult. During a period when our kids need to detach from us, we can at least support them by helping them find a college that supports this vulnerable period of metamorphosis.

As Loren Pope advised in his classic, *Colleges That Change Lives*, families should seek out schools with "a familial sense of communal enterprise... and a faculty of scholars devoted to helping young people develop their powers, mentors who often become their valued friends."[6]

As for parents entering our own liminal phase, we need guides too. We all need a "Yoda,"[7] whether that be a psychotherapist, pastoral counselor, wise friend, or insightful author (one of my own favorite guidebooks is *Finding Meaning in the Second Half of Life* by Jungian analyst James Hollis[8]). As long as we are living, we are evolving and in the words of Carl Jung, *individuating*. The exciting adventure continues: we are all *"forever Jung"*!

53. College Freshmen Home for Thanksgiving

Homecoming unites the past and the present.

-Anonymous

It's yet another rite of passage for college freshmen.

For some, it is the first time they will be home since they left for college in August. For others, it is the first time they will see their core group of high school friends. For all, it's an opportunity to touch base with "the mother ship" before final exams, feasting on nostalgic comfort food during football halftime. And a time for "taking stock" of their freshman experience so far. What to expect? Change.

Your returning young adult is not the high school student you moved into the dorm in August. Your son or daughter has gone through an enormous level of change! Your freshman has taken many steps toward independent adulthood, ranging from waking on his or her own (without your nagging) to returning at night when he or she chooses (without asking permission, a curfew, or "reporting in" to anyone).

Do your son or daughter and favor by avoiding obnoxious parentisms described from a student's point of view in the hilarious article "Welcome Home, Honey!" at CollegeCandy.com.[1]

How will you deal with these changes? You know you can't freeze him in time; you must respect his new autonomy. But you also have a right to boundaries at home.

A curfew, or at least agreement on when he will come home, is appropriate for holiday visits. Returning to the dorm at 4:00 a.m. may be OK, but not at home where a night owl's schedule clashes with parents and siblings. Campus security may ignore rowdy students wandering in the wee hours, but suburban police will not. This is a great time to distinguish between college and home "house rules."

Your freshman may be surprised that he is not the only one who has gone through changes. Parents and siblings change too. Family dynamics are altered when a key player has been removed from the scene. The freshman's return may conflict with new patterns that are just being established. It may take time for everyone to readjust.

As a parent, you may desire more "rebonding" than fits the comfort level of your freshman who would rather go out with friends than sit at the dinner table and recount his college experience with you *ad nauseam*. Or, if you've just become an empty nester, you may be surprised at how quickly you've become used to your own independence from parenthood. You're not geared to "waiting up" at night anymore, twiddling your thumbs until you hear his or her car in the driveway. You no longer have patience for picking up half-empty soda cans everywhere in the family room, as endearing as they are.

Thanksgiving is classically known as a time of truth for freshmen reconnecting with high school friends. For many, this first semester is characterized by friendsickness, a grieving period for friends from home. Finally having a face-to-face meeting with old friends offers reassurance that some pals are "keepers," or the realization that it is time to "move on" from other friendships.

Dating relationships often come to a pivotal inflection point now. Freshmen with long-distance relationships with high school sweethearts may decide to continue exclusively, date only when both are home, break up altogether (known as the "turkey drop"), or morph into a friendship. Parents need to remember that there is no "right" outcome: each relationship will run its natural course.

Be prepared for anything when your young adult comes home, from physical changes such as the "Freshman Fifteen" [2] to evidence of emotional crises (anxiety, depression, eating disorders, substance abuse). A good primer on recognizing adolescents' psychological issues is College of the *Overwhelmed: The Campus Mental Health Crisis and What to Do about It* by Richard Kadison and Theresa Foy DiGeronimo.[3] If you were too scared to buy it before college, read *Binge: What Your College Student Won't Tell You* by Barrett Seaman, for a reality check about alcohol excess and other toxic elements of college life.[4] *Knowing is better than not knowing.*

It should not surprise you if your freshman does not return from college in a state of bliss, as you may have envisioned during the toughest months of the college process. At the beginning of this book, I referenced the *New York Times'* article: "Record Level of Stress Found in College Freshmen, Survey Finds," based on a study finding that only 52 percent of first-year college students said their emotional health was above average, versus 64 percent in 1985.[5] Remember William Damon's finding, discussed in his book, *The Path to Purpose: Helping Our Children Find Their Calling in Life,* that a quarter of adolescents interviewed were rudderless, grappling with "purposelessness."[5]

Does this mean your adolescent's college-bound journey actually has been a *Race to Nowhere* [6]?

It is far too early to make any such pronouncement. A young person's life is a movie, not a snapshot. One year of confusion or unhappiness may actually lead to greater insight and direction the following year. We cannot overreact to our children's state of mind at any single point in time. I feel that we must keep listening, guiding, caring, and believing in them, modeling a sense of purpose ourselves. We won't solve this one over a single holiday weekend, that's for sure. It's always a moving target, an evolving journey, a work-in-progress.

Be ready for Thanksgiving bombshells, such as "I want to transfer." This is actually quite common, if a student does not yet feel connected with new friends, is somewhat disillusioned by the college experience, or is beginning to sense a mismatch between his goals and the school's programs.

Dr. Allen Grove, director of a program to help students transition to college, wrote two excellent articles about "good" and "bad" reasons to transfer in About.com. His five "good" reasons are: financial necessity, academic upgrade, specialized major, family obligations, or social situation. Five "bad" reasons: love, your school is too hard, you're homesick, you hate your roommate, or you hate your professors.[7]

This is a time to listen carefully and heartfully. For now, I recommend a wait-and-see attitude, underscoring the need for strong academic performance to maximize transfer flexibility. Often the student feels better by spring and the transfer idea dissipates. If the transfer need is real, it will persist, in which case, your son or daughter will *still* glad he or she earned that strong academic record.

One thing that does not change is your family pet's eagerness to welcome your freshman home. When our son returned that first Thanksgiving, our two Shelties were thrilled, especially the older one who grew up with him. Like the patriarchal golden retriever Shadow in *Homeward Bound: The Incredible Journey*[8], our old Blaze became a puppy again when reunited with "his boy."

In Eric's sophomore year, his beloved canine companion turned fourteen. In fact, wise old Blaze chose that day for his own passing: his fourteenth birthday was also the day after our son returned to Emory following winter break.

Somehow Blaze seemed to know that "his boy" was becoming independent, approaching that original goal of honorable adulthood. A class act till the end, he knew it was time for him to go.

VII. End Notes

My Story

1. Kris Hintz, "NJ College Admissions Consultant & Coach, NJ College Adviser, College Admissions Coach New Jersey Â– Position U 4 College ," NJ College Admissions Consultant & Coach, NJ College Adviser, College Admissions Coach New Jersey Â– Position U 4 College, http://www.positionu4college.com/.

2. Kris Hintz, "Collegeblog by Kris Hintz," Collegeblog by Kris Hintz. http://positionu4college.wordpress.com/.

3. Kris Hintz, "Careerblog by Kris Hintz," Careerblog by Kris Hintz, http://positionu4life.wordpress.com/.

1. Honorable Adulthood

1. "The Civil War (TV series) - Wikipedia, the Free Encyclopedia," Wikipedia, the Free Encyclopedia, http://en.wikipedia.org/wiki/The_Civil_War_%28TV_series%29, accessed January 13, 2011.

2. "The Civil War. The Film. Music of the Civil War | PBS," PBS: Public Broadcasting Service, http://www.pbs.org/civilwar/film/music.html, accessed January 13, 2011.

3. "The Civil War, The War, Historical Documents: Sullivan Ballou Letter | PBS," PBS: Public Broadcasting Service, accessed January 28, 2011, http://www.pbs.org/civilwar/war/ballou_letter.html.

4. Foster W. Cline and Jim Fay, *Parenting with Love and Logic: Teaching Children Responsibility*, (CO: Pinon Press, 1990).

5. Robert A. Heinlein, *Time Enough for Love*, (New York: Putnam, 1973).

6. "Famous Quotes by Roseanne Barr | Quotes Daddy," 1,000,000 Famous Quotes and Quotations | QuotesDaddy, accessed January 13, 2011, http://www.quotesdaddy.com/author/Roseanne+Barr.

2. What's Important to Colleges? Top Ten Factors

1. Melissa Clinedinst and David Hawkins, "State of College Admission 2010 Report," NACACNet, accessed January 28, 2011, http://www.nacanet.org/PublicationsResources/marketplace/research/Pages/StateofCollegeAdmission.aspx.

3. Public versus Private Universities or Liberal Arts Colleges

1. "Public University - Wikipedia, the Free Encyclopedia," Wikipedia, The Free Encyclopedia, http://en.wikipedia.org/wiki/Public_university, accessed March 5, 2011.

2. "Public University - Wikipedia, the Free Encyclopedia," Wikipedia, The Free Encyclopedia, http://en.wikipedia.org/wiki/Public_university, accessed March 5, 2011.

3. "Encyclopedia Britannica - Wikipedia, the Free Encyclopedia," Wikipedia, The Free Encyclopedia, http://en.wikipedia.org/wiki/Encyclop%C3%A6dia_Britannica, accessed March 5, 2011.

4. "Liberal Arts - Wikipedia, the Free Encyclopedia," Wikipedia, The Free Encyclopedia, http://en.wikipedia.org/wiki/Liberal_arts, accessed March 5, 2011.

5. "Binghamton University - Admission: Undergraduate Admission: Costs and Financial Aid: Affording Binghamton," Bing-

hamton University – Home, http://www2.binghamton.edu/admissions/attendance-costs.html, accessed March 5, 2011.

6. "Best Values in Public Colleges, 2010-11," Kiplinger - Personal Finance, Business, Investing, Retirement, and Financial Advice, http://www.kiplinger.com/tools/colleges/, accessed March 5, 2011.

7. "College Compass," US News & World Report College Compass, premium.usnews.com/best-colleges/rankings/national-universities/data, accessed March 5, 2011.

8. Richard Arum and Josipa Roksa, *Academically Adrift Limited Learning on College Campuses*, (Chicago: University Of Chicago Press, 2011).

9. "College Compass," US News & World Report College Compass, premium.usnews.com/best-colleges/rankings/national-universities/data, accessed March 5, 2011.

10. Melissa Clinedinst and David Hawkins, "State of College Admission 2010 Report," NACACNet, accessed January 28, 2011, http://www.nacanet.org/PublicationsResources/marketplace/research/Pages/StateofCollegeAdmission.aspx.

4. Do You Need a Passion to Get into College?

1. "Urban Dictionary: passion." Urban Dictionary, March 4: going ham. http://www.urbandictionary.com/define.php?term=passion (accessed March 4, 2010).

5. Your Target Colleges--And It's a Moving Target

1. Jacques Steinberg, "Top Colleges Have Bigger Waiting Lists - NYTimes.com," The New York Times - Breaking News, World News & Multimedia, http://www.nytimes.com/2010/04/14/education/14waitlist.html?_r=1.

2. Daniel de Vise, "College Wait Lists Grow as Schools Hedge Bets on Enrollment Numbers," Washington Post - Politics, National,

World & D.C. Area News and Headlines - washingtonpost.com. http://www.washingtonpost.com/wp-dyn/content/article/2010/05/14/AR2010051403691.html.

3. "College Compass," US News & World Report College Compass, premium.usnews.com/best-colleges/rankings/national-universities/data, accessed March 5, 2011.

4. George Keller, *Transforming a College: The Story of a Little Known College's Strategic Climb to National Distinction*, (Baltimore: The Johns Hopkins University Press, 2004).

5. Loren Pope, *Colleges That Change Lives: 40 Schools That Will Change the Way You Think About Colleges*, (New York: Penguin Books, 2006).

6. Everybody Needs a Tiger

1. Chua, Amy. *Battle Hymn of the Tiger Mother*. (USA: The Penguin Press, 2011).

2. *The Miracle Worker*, Directed by Arthur Penn, (Pittsburgh: MGM), 1962, DVD.

3. Carol Fishman Cohen, "In Japan and Korea, Asian-style Parenting Means Mom Stays Home," Working Mother, accessed January 28, 2011, http://www.workingmother.com/BestCompanies/thought-leaders/2011/01/in-japan-and-korea-asian-style-parenting-means-mom-stays-home.

4. Hillary Rodham Clinton, *It Takes a Village*, (New York: Simon & Schuster, 1996).

5. Robert Brooks, Ph.D. and Sam Goldstein, Ph.D., *Raising Resilient Children: Fostering Strength, Hope, and Optimism, in Your Child*, (Chicago: Contemporary Books, 2001).

6. Robert Brooks, Ph.D., "Education and 'Charismatic' Adults: To Touch a Student's Heart and Mind," Psychologist, Motivational Speaker, and Author on Resilience, Motivation, and

Family Relationships: Dr. Robert Brooks, accessed January 28, 2011, http://www.drrobertbrooks.com/writings/articles/0009.html.

7. A College Consultant's Grown-Up Christmas List

1. Amy Grant, vocal performance of "Grown-Up Christmas List," by David Foster and Linda Thompson Jenner with additional verse by Amy Grant, produced by Brown Bannister, released October 6, 1992, on *Home for Christmas Amy Grant*, A&M Records, Inc., 7502846, compact disc.

2. Sally P Springer et al, *Admission Matters: What Students and Parents Need to Know About Getting into College, Mobipocket Edition*, (San Francisco, CA: Jossey-Bass, 2009).

3. Springer et al, *Admission*, 215.

4. "Number of educational institutions, by level and control of institution: Selected years, 1980–81 through 2004–05," National Center for Education Statistics (NCES) Home Page, a part of the U.S. Department of Education, accessed December 26, 2010, http://nces.ed.gov/programs/digest/d06/tables/dt06_005.asp.

5. "Number of Educational Institutions, by Level and Control of Institution: Selected Years, 1980–81 through 2004–05," National Center for Education Statistics (NCES) Home Page, a part of the U.S. Department of Education, accessed December 26, 2010, http://nces.ed.gov/programs/digest/d06/tables/dt06_005.asp.

6. Anthony J. Onwuegbuzie and Michael A. Seaman, "The Effect of Time Constraints and Statistics Test Anxiety on Test Performance in a Statistics Course by Anthony J. Onwuegbuzie," Questia - The Online Library of Books and Journals, accessed December 26, 2010, http://www.questia.com/read/98487204?title=The percent20Effect percent20of percent20Time percent20Constraints percent20and

percent20Statistics percent20Test percent20Anxiety percent20on percent20Test percent20Performance percent20in percent20a percent20Statistics percent20Course.

8. College Consultants? Who Needs 'Em?

1. "Research & Statistics - ED.gov," U.S. Department of Education, accessed June 7, 2010, http://ed.gov/rschstat/landing.jhtml.

2. "Marketplace," NACAC Homepage, accessed June 7, 2010, http://www.nacacnet.org/PublicationsResources/Marketplace/Pages/default.aspx.

3. Sally P Springer et al, *Admission Matters: What Students and Parents Need to Know About Getting into College, Mobipocket Edition*, (San Francisco, CA: Jossey-Bass, 2009).

4. Springer et al, *Admission*, 2.

5. Springer et al, *Admission*, 3.

6. Springer et al, *Admission*, 3-4.

9. How to Afford College

1. "Family Finance, Financial Planning, Budgeting, Managing Money – Kiplinger," Kiplinger - Personal Finance, Business, Investing, Retirement, and Financial Advice, accessed May 6, 2010, http://www.kiplinger.com/family-finance/.

2. "MeritAid.com: Search Merit Scholarships, Academic Scholarships, Merit Awards - Merit Aid – Search," MeritAid.com: Search Merit Scholarships, Academic Scholarships, Merit Awards - Merit Aid – Search, accessed May 6, 2010, http://www.meritaid.com/.

3. Mariah Balaban and Jennifer Shields, *Study Away: The Unauthorized Guide to College Abroad*, (New York: Anchor Books, 2003).

4. "College Compass," US News & World Report College Compass, premium.usnews.com/best-colleges/rankings/national-universities/data, accessed March 5, 2011.

5. "Winter 2010 Survey of Community College Presidents | The Campus Computing Project," The Campus Computing Project, accessed May 6, 2010, http://www.campuscomputing.net/winter-2010-survey-community-college-presidents.

6. Lynn O'Shaughnessy, *The College Solution: A Guide for Everyone Looking for the Right School at the Right Price*, (NJ: FT Press, 2008).

7. "FastWeb : Scholarships, Financial Aid, Student Loans and Colleges," Fastweb : Scholarships, Financial Aid, Student Loans and Colleges, accessed May 6, 2010, http://www.fastweb.com/.

8. Benjamin R. Kaplan, *How to Go to College Almost for Free: The Secrets of Winning Scholarship Money*, 2nd ed., (New York: Harper Resource, 2002).

9. "Upromise How it Works, Earn Money for College with Everyday Purchases," Upromise Welcome, Money for College through Shopping Online, eCoupons, Grocery, Restaurants, Upromise Credit Card, $ Finance, Auto, Home, & More, accessed May 6, 2010, http://www.upromise.com/welcome/how-it-works.

10. Tim Higgins, *Pay for College Without Sacrificing Your Retirement: A Guide to Your Financial Future*, (Point Richmond, California: Bay Tree Publishing, 2008).

11. "FinAid! Financial Aid, College Scholarships and Student Loans," FinAid! Financial Aid, College Scholarships and Student Loans, accessed May 6, 2010, http://www.finaid.org/.

10. The Race to Nowhere and the Path to Purpose

1. *Race to Nowhere*, Directed by Vicki H. Abeles, (Lafayette, CA: Reel Link Films), 2010, DVD.

2. "Race to Nowhere | About the Film," Race to Nowhere | Changing Lives One Film at a Time, accessed February 5, 2011, http://www.racetonowhere.com/about-film.

3. Melissa Clinedinst and David Hawkins, "State of College Admission 2010 Report," NACACNet, accessed January 28, 2011, http://www.nacanet.org/PublicationsResources/marketplace/research/Pages/StateofCollegeAdmission.aspx.

4. "Number of Educational Institutions, by Level and Control of Institution: Selected Years, 1980–81 through 2004–05," National Center for Education Statistics (NCES) Home Page, a part of the U.S. Department of Education, accessed December 26, 2010, http://nces.ed.gov/programs/digest/d06/tables/dt06_005.asp.

5. Tamar Lewin, "College Freshmen Stress Levels High, Survey Finds - NYTimes.com," The New York Times - Breaking News, World News & Multimedia, accessed February 5, 2011, http://www.nytimes.com/2011/01/27/education/27colleges.html?_r=1.

6. "Higher Education Research Institute (HERI) - HERI Home," Higher Education Research Institute (HERI) - HERI Home, accessed February 5, 2011, http://www.heri.ucla.edu/index.php.

7. Madeline Levine, *The Price of Privilege: How Parental Pressure and Material Advantage Are Creating a Generation of Disconnected and Unhappy Kids*, (New York: Harper Collins, 2006).

8. Levine, *Privilege,* Kindle edition, 881-906.

9. William Damon, *The Path to Purpose: How Young People Find Their Calling in Life*, (New York: Free Press, 2009).

10. Damon, *Purpose*, Kindle edition, 914-927.

11. Loren Pope, *Colleges That Change Lives: 40 Schools That Will Change the Way You Think About Colleges*, (New York: Penguin Books, 2006).

11. Not Just Getting into College: Parenting for Purpose

1. *City Slickers.* Directed by Ron Underwood, (United States: Columbia Pictures), 1991, DVD.

2. William Damon, The Path to Purpose: How Young People Find Their Calling in Life, (New York: Free Press, 2009).

3. Damon, *Purpose*, Kindle edition, 914-927.

4. Damon, *Purpose*, Kindle edition, 1774-2215.

5. "Ryan's Well Foundation | About Us," Ryan's Well Foundation | Home, http://www.ryanswell.ca/about-us.aspx, accessed February 23, 2011.

6. "Little Kids Rock," Little Kids Rock, http://littlekidsrock.org/what-we-do.html, accessed February 23, 2011.

7. "Swim with the Dolphins at Dolphin Research Center Marathon FL, Dolphin and Sea Lion Research," Swim with the Dolphins at Dolphin Research Center Marathon FL, Dolphin and Sea Lion Research, http://www.dolphins.org/, accessed February 23, 2011.

8. Jared Sandberg, "Explaining 'VP, Biz Dev' to Your Kid - The Juggle – WSJ," WSJ Blogs – WSJ, http://blogs.wsj.com/juggle/2007/07/11/explaining-vp-biz-dev-to-your-kid/, accessed February 23, 2011.

9. "Washington Semester American University Washington, DC," Washington Semester American University Home, www.american.edu/washingtonsemester/, accessed February 23, 2011.

10. *Dead Poets Society (Special Edition)*, Directed by Peter Weir, (Hartford: Buena Vista Home Entertainment / Touchstone), 1989, DVD.

11. James Hillman, *The Soul's Code: In Search of Character and Calling*, (New York: Random House, 1996).

12. The First Day of High School

1. Barbara Strauch, *The Primal Teen: What the New Discoveries about the Teenage Brain Tell Us about Our Kids*, (New York: Doubleday, 2003).

2. Anthony E. Wolf, Ph.D., *Get Out of My Life, but First Could You Drive Me and Cheryl to the Mall?: A Parent's Guide to the New Teenager*, First Revised ed. (New York: Farrar, Straus, & Giroux Books, 2002).

3. "Class Schedule - High School Courses - English, Math, Social Studies," College Admissions - SAT - University & College Search Tool, accessed August 31, 2009, http://www.college-board.com/student/plan/high-school/33.html.

4. Melissa Clinedinst and David Hawkins, "State of College Admission 2010 Report," NACACNet, accessed January 28, 2011, http://www.nacanet.org/PublicationsResources/marketplace/research/Pages/StateofCollegeAdmission.aspx.

5. *Race to Nowhere*, Directed by Vicki H. Abeles, (Lafayette, CA: Reel Link Films), 2010, DVD.

6. "Family Finance, Financial Planning, Budgeting, Managing Money – Kiplinger," Kiplinger - Personal Finance, Business,

Investing, Retirement, and Financial Advice, accessed May 6, 2010, http://www.kiplinger.com/family-finance/.

7. Lynn O'Shaughnessy, "The College Solution Blog," The College Solution Blog, accessed August 31, 2009, http://www. thecollegesolutionblog.com/.

13. Ten Things You Can Do for Your College-Bound Tenth Grader

1. Sandra L. Berger, *The Ultimate Guide to Summer Opportunities for Teens: 200 Programs That Prepare You for College Success,* (Waco, Tex.: Prufrock Press, 2008).

2. Damon, *Purpose,* Kindle edition, 1774-2215.

3. *Race to Nowhere,* Directed by Vicki H. Abeles, (Lafayette, CA: Reel Link Films), 2010, DVD.

14. High School Testing Strategy and Timeline

1. "SAT Percentile Ranks, 2010 College-Bound Seniors Critical Reading, Mathematics, and Writing Percentile Ranks," College Board, accessed November 8, 2010, http://professionals.collegeboard.com/profdownload/sat-percentile-ranks-2010.pdf.

2. "National Merit Scholarship Corporation – NMSP," National Merit Scholarship Corporation, accessed November 8, 2010, http://www.nationalmerit.org/nmsp.php.

3. "Compass SAT Subject Tests FAQ," Compass Education Group, accessed November 8, 2010, http://www.compassprep.com/ subject_faq.shtml#faq19.

4. "Compass: Admissions Requirements," Compass Education Group, accessed November 8, 2010, http://www.compassprep.com/admissions_req_subjects.aspx.

5. "Optional List | FairTest," The National Center for Fair & Open Testing | FairTest, accessed November 8, 2010, http://www. fairtest.org/university/optional.

16. Ten Ways for Teens to Spend the Summer

1. Alex Altman, "A Brief History Of: Summer Vacation – TIME," Breaking News, Analysis, Politics, Blogs, News Photos, Video, Tech Reviews - TIME.com, accessed May 20, 2009, http://www. time.com/time/magazine/article/0,9171,1816501,00.html.

2. Sandra L. Berger, *The Ultimate Guide to Summer Opportunities for Teens: 200 Programs That Prepare You for College Success*, (Waco, Tex.: Prufrock Press, 2008).

3. Kristin M. White, *The Complete Guide to the Gap Year: The Best Things to Do Between High School and College, Mobipocket Edition.*, (San Francisco, CA: Jossey-Bass, 2009).

4. "LeadAmerica Youth Leadership Programs | Academic Summer Programs for High School Students | College Readiness," LeadAmerica Youth Leadership Programs | Academic Summer Programs for High School Students | College Readiness, accessed May 20, 2009, http://www.lead-america.org/.

5. "Broadreach Teen Summer Camps. Scuba Camps, Caribbean Sailing Camps, Marine Biology, Teen Travel, Wilderness Summer Programs," Broadreach Teen Summer Camps. Scuba Camps, Caribbean Sailing Camps, Marine Biology, Teen Travel, Wilderness Summer Programs, accessed May 20, 2009, http://www.gobroadreach.com/.

6. "Teen Adventure Travel | Summer Programs Abroad | Adventure Camps for Teens," Teen Adventure Travel | Summer Programs Abroad | Adventure Camps for Teens, accessed May 20, 2009, http://www.overlandsummers.com/.

7. "Where There Be Dragons: Summer & Semester Study Abroad Programs for High School & College Students in Asia,

Africa & Americas," Where There Be Dragons: Summer & Semester Study Abroad Programs for High School & College Students in Asia, Africa & Americas, accessed May 20, 2009, http://www.wheretherebedragons.com/.

8. "Habitat for Humanity Int'l," Habitat for Humanity Int'l, accessed May 20, 2009, http://www.habitat.org/.

9. "Congressional Award: Congress' Award for Youth," Congressional Award: Congress' Award for Youth, accessed May 20, 2009, http://www.congressionalaward.org/.

10. "National Honor Society and National Junior Honor Society - NHS & NJHS," National Honor Society and National Junior Honor Society - NHS & NJHS, accessed May 20, 2009, http://www.nhs.us/.

11. "Welcome to the Eagle Scout Resource Center at EagleScout.Org!," Welcome to the Eagle Scout Resource Center at EagleScout.Org!, accessed May 20, 2009, http://www.eaglescout.org/.

12. "GS Central: Girl Scout Gold Award," Girl Scouts of the USA: Official Web Site, accessed May 20, 2009, http://www.girlscouts.org/program/gs_central/insignia/highest_awards/gold_award.asp.

13. *Race to Nowhere*, Directed by Vicki H. Abeles, (Lafayette, CA: Reel Link Films), 2010, DVD.

17. Your Eleventh Graders Eleven Steps to Success

1. "National Merit Scholarship Corporation," National Merit Scholarship Corporation, accessed August 6, 2009, http://www.nationalmerit.org/index.php.

18. Calendar for High School Juniors

1. "Video Gallery - The Ellen DeGeneres Show," The Ellen DeGeneres Show: The Place for Ellen Tickets, Celebrity Photos, Videos, Games, Giveaways and More. accessed December 8, 2010, http://ellen.warnerbros.com/videos/?autoplay=true& mediaKey=87584a4b-88d6-4715-85d3-e4c7fe8e8f2d.

19. Parents of Eleventh Graders: Get Set for "Junior College Night!"

1. Sally P Springer et al, *Admission Matters: What Students and Parents Need to Know About Getting into College, Mobipocket Edition,* (San Francisco, CA: Jossey-Bass, 2009).

2. Springer et al, *Admission,* 2.

3. Springer et al, *Admission,* 3.

4. Springer et al, *Admission,* 3-4.

5. Springer et al, *Admission,* 5.

20. College Reading List for Eleventh Grade Parents

1. Lynn O'Shaughnessy, *The College Solution: A Guide for Everyone Looking for the Right School at the Right Price,* (NJ: FT Press, 2008).

2. Sally P Springer et al, *Admission Matters: What Students and Parents Need to Know About Getting into College, Mobipocket Edition,* (San Francisco, CA: Jossey-Bass, 2009).

3. Howard Greene and Matthew W. Greene, *The Hidden Ivies, 2nd Edition: 50 Top Colleges - from Amherst to Williams - That Rival the Ivy League,* (New York: Harper Collins Publishers, 2009).

4. Loren Pope, *Colleges That Change Lives: 40 Schools That Will Change the Way You Think About Colleges,* (New York: Penguin Books, 2006).

5. Michele A. Hernández, *A Is for Admission: The Insider's Guide to Getting Into the Ivy League and Other Top Colleges*. (New York: Warner Books, 1997).

6. Tim Higgins, *Pay for College Without Sacrificing Your Retirement: A Guide to Your Financial Future*, (Point Richmond, California: Bay Tree Publishing, 2008).

7. Steven R. Antonoff, *College Match: A Blueprint for Choosing the Best School for You!*, 5th ed., (Alexandria, VA: Octameron Associates, 1997).

8. Steven R. Antonoff, *The College Finder: Choose the School That's Right for You!*, 3rd ed. (Westford, MA: Wintergreen Orchard House, 2008).

9. "College Rankings & Scholarships | InsideCollege.com," College Rankings & Scholarships | InsideCollege.com, accessed October 4, 2010, http://www.insidecollege.com/reno/home. do.

10. Sandra L. Berger, *The Ultimate Guide to Summer Opportunities for Teens: 200 Programs That Prepare You for College Success*, (Waco, Tex.: Prufrock Press, 2008).

11. Yale Daily News Staff, *The Insider's Guide to the Colleges, 2011: Students on Campus Tell You What You Really Want to Know, 37th Edition*, (New Haven, CT: The Yale Daily News Publishing Company, 2011).

12. Yale, *Guide*.

21. Preparing for the SAT: "E" for Effort

1. Claudia Buchmann et al, "(Page 1 of 23) - The Myth of Meritocracy? SAT Preparation, College Enrollment, Class and Race in the United States authored by Buchmann, Claudia, Roscigno, Vincent. and Condron, Dennis," All Academic Inc. (Abstract Management, Conference Management and

Research Search Engine), accessed November 9, 2010, http://www.allacademic.com//meta/p_mla_apa_research_citation/1/0/4/5/5/pages104558/p104558-1.php.

2. Dr. K. Anders Ericsson, "Dr. K. Anders Ericsson," Psychology at Florida State University, accessed November 9, 2010, http://www.psy.fsu.edu/faculty/ericsson.dp.html.

22. Should I Take the SAT, the ACT, or BOTH?

1. "About Us - The College Board," About Us - The College Board, accessed November 7, 2010, http://about.collegeboard.org/.

2. "About ACT | ACT Company Profile | ACT," ACT | Helping People Achieve Education and Workplace Success, accessed November 7, 2010, http://www.act.org/aboutact/profile. html.

3. Steve Vogel, "College Admissions: SAT vs. ACT: Which Test to Take? Learn the Differences Between the Two," Suite101.com: Online Magazine and Writers' Network, accessed November 7, 2010, http://www.suite101.com/content/college-admissions-sat-vs-act-a35051.

4. Steve Vogel, "College Admissions: SAT vs. ACT: Which Test to Take? Learn the Differences Between the Two," Suite101.com: Online Magazine and Writers' Network, accessed November 7, 2010, http://www.suite101.com/content/college-admissions-sat-vs-act-a35051.

5. Steve Vogel, "College Admissions: SAT vs. ACT: Which Test to Take? Learn the Differences Between the Two," Suite101.com: Online Magazine and Writers' Network, accessed November 7, 2010, http://www.suite101.com/content/college-admissions-sat-vs-act-a35051.

6. "ACT-SAT Concordance," ACT | Helping People Achieve Education and Workplace Success, accessed November 7, 2010, http://www.act.org/aap/concordance/.

23. High School Juniors Apathetic about College Applications?

1. Barbara Strauch, *The Primal Teen: What the New Discoveries about the Teenage Brain Tell Us about Our Kids*, (New York: Doubleday, 2003).

24. I'll Only Visit the Colleges I Get Into

1. Jacques Steinberg, "College Students' Transfer Rate Is About 1 in 3 - NYTimes.com," College Admissions Advice - The Choice Blog - NYTimes.com, accessed June 15, 2010, http://thechoice.blogs.nytimes.com/2010/04/27/transfer/.

2. Peter Schworm, "Colleges Favoring Applicants Who Show Keen Interest - The Boston Globe," Boston.com, accessed June 15, 2010, http://www.boston.com/news/education/higher/articles/2009/03/15/a_new_factor_in_making_that_college_loving_it/.

27. Finding the Best College for Your Major

1. Steven R. Antonoff, *The College Finder: Choose the School That's Right for You!*, 3rd ed. (Westford, MA: Wintergreen Orchard House, 2008).

2. "College Rankings & Scholarships | InsideCollege.com," College Rankings & Scholarships | InsideCollege.com, accessed January 23, 2010, http://www.insidecollege.com/reno/home.do.

3. College Board, *Book of Majors 2011 (College Board Book of Majors)*, (New York: College Board Publications, 2011).

4. Elaina Loveland, *Creative Colleges: A Guide for Student Actors, Artists, Dancers, Musicians and Writers*, (Belmont, CA: SuperCollege, LLC, 2005).

5. Edward Schoenberg and Kevin Buck, *A Guide to College Choices for the Performing and Visual Arts*, (Raleigh, NC: Lulu.com, 2008.)

6. "College Compass," US News & World Report College Compass, premium.usnews.com/best-colleges/rankings/national-universities/data, accessed March 5, 2011.

7. "Trends, Strategies, Research for Design Professionals: DesignIntelligence," Trends, Strategies, Research for Design Professionals: DesignIntelligence, accessed January 23, 2010, http://www.di.net/.

8. Edward Keegan, "The Top 10 U.S. Undergraduate Degree Programs in Architecture - Students, Education, Architecture - Architect Magazine," Architect Magazine: Architectural Design | Architect Online: A premier site for Architecture Industry News & Building Resources, accessed January 23, 2010, http://www.architectmagazine.com/architecture/the-undergraduate-programs.aspx.

28. Preparing for College Essays by Journaling

1. Trip Gabriel, "The Almighty Essay Is a Tough Assignment - NYTimes.com," The New York Times - Breaking News, World News & Multimedia, accessed January 30, 2011, http://www.nytimes.com/2011/01/09/education/09guidance-t.html?_r=1.

30. Tricks and Treats of the Common Application

1. "The Common Application," The Common Application, accessed October 30, 2010, https://www.commonapp.org/CommonApp/default.aspx.

2. Melissa Clinedinst and David Hawkins, "State of College Admission 2010 Report," NACACNet, accessed January 28, 2011, http://www.nacanet.org/PublicationsResources/marketplace/research/Pages/StateofCollegeAdmission.aspx.

32. How Important Is the College Essay, Really?

1. Melissa Clinedinst and David Hawkins, "State of College Admission 2010 Report," NACACNet, accessed January

28, 2011, http://www.nacanet.org/PublicationsResources/
marketplace/research/Pages/StateofCollegeAdmission.
aspx.

34. "Confessional" College Essays

1. Don Dunbar et al, *What You Don't Know Can Keep You Out of College: A Top Consultant Explains the 13 Fatal Application Mistakes and Why Character Is the Key to College Admissions*, (New York, N.Y.: Gotham Books, 2007).

2. Dunbar et al, *Know*, 59.

35. Why "University of X?" College Essay

1. Melissa Clinedinst and David Hawkins, "State of College Admission 2010 Report," NACACNet, accessed January 28, 2011, http://www.nacanet.org/PublicationsResources/ marketplace/research/Pages/StateofCollegeAdmission. aspx.

2. Peter Schworm, "Colleges Favoring Applicants Who Show Keen Interest - The Boston Globe," Boston.com, accessed June 15, 2010, http://www.boston.com/news/education/ higher/articles/2009/03/15/a_new_factor_in_making_that_ college_loving_it/.

37. December College News

1. Sally P Springer et al, *Admission Matters: What Students and Parents Need to Know About Getting into College, Mobipocket Edition,* (San Francisco, CA: Jossey-Bass, 2009).

2. Springer et al, *Admission*, 214.

3. Springer et al, *Admission*, 214.

4. Springer et al, *Admission*, 214.

5. Springer et al, *Admission*, 215.

6. Michele A. Hernández, *A Is for Admission: The Insider's Guide to Getting Into the Ivy League and Other Top Colleges.* (New York: Warner Books, 1997).

7. Hernández, *Ivy,* 38.

8. Springer et al, *Admission,* 216.

9. Hernández, *Ivy,* 39-41.

10. "Naviance - The Leading Provider of K-12 Solutions that Inspire Students to Achieve Post-Secondary Success," Naviance -The Leading Provider of K-12 Solutions that Inspire Students to Achieve Post-Secondary Success, accessed December 1, 2009, http://www.naviance.com/.

11. Springer et al, *Admission,* 215.

38. Waiting for the Fat Envelope

1. Sally P Springer et al, *Admission Matters: What Students and Parents Need to Know About Getting into College, Mobipocket Edition,* (San Francisco, CA: Jossey-Bass, 2009).

2. Springer et al, *Admission,* 224.

3. Springer et al, *Admission,* 226.

4. Springer et al, *Admission,* 226-27.

5. Springer et al, *Admission,* 227.

39. Dealing with Rejection

1. "Social Rejection - Wikipedia, the Free Encyclopedia," Wikipedia, the Free Encyclopedia, http://en.wikipedia.org/wiki/Social_rejection, accessed April 9, 2011.

2. "Study Illuminates the 'Pain' of Social Rejection," Science Daily: News & Articles in Science, Health, Environment &

Technology, accessed April 9, 2011, http://www.sciencedaily. com/releases/2011/03/110328151726.htm.

3. "Jean Piaget - Wikipedia, the Free Encyclopedia," Wikipedia, the Free Encyclopedia, accessed April 9, 2011, http://en.wikipedia.org/wiki/Jean_Piaget.

4. "Welcome to All Things Human!," Welcome to All Things Human!, accessed April 9, 2011, http://www.allthingshuman. net/index.php?.

5. "Iroise Dumontheil | Karolinska Institute - Academia.edu," Karolinska Institute - Academia.edu, accessed April 9, 2011, http://ki.academia.edu/IroiseDumontheil.

6. "Welcome to All Things Human!," Welcome to All Things Human!, accessed April 9, 2011, http://www.allthingshuman. net/index.php?.

7. David Crary, "Study Finds Students Narcissistic - Boston.com," Featured Articles From Boston.com, accessed April 9, 2011, http://articles.boston.com/2007-02-27/news/29231950_1_ college-students-study-.

8. Jean M. and W. Keith Campbell, The Narcissism Epidemic: Living in the Age of Entitlement, (New York: Free Press, 2009).

9. Mark Bauerlein, "Teen Narcissism - Brainstorm - The Chronicle of Higher Education," Home - The Chronicle of Higher Education, accessed April 9, 2011, http://chronicle.com/blogs/ brainstorm/teen-narcissism/6535,

10. "Magical Thinking - Wikipedia, the Free Encyclopedia," Wikipedia, the Free Encyclopedia, accessed April 9, 2011, http:// en.wikipedia.org/wiki/Magical_thinking.

11. Michele A. Hernández, A Is for Admission: The Insider's Guide to Getting Into the Ivy League and Other Top Colleges, (New York: Warner Books, 1997).

12. Mitchell L. Stevens, Creating a Class: College Admissions and the Education of Elites, (Cambridge, Mass.: Harvard University Press, 2007). \

13. Gregg Easterbrook, The Progress Paradox: How Life Gets Better While People Feel Worse, (New York: Random House, 2003).

14. Tom Brokaw, The Greatest Generation, (New York: Random House, 1998).

15. "Cognitive Distortion - Wikipedia, the Free Encyclopedia," Wikipedia, the Free Encyclopedia, accessed April 9, 2011, http://en.wikipedia.org/wiki/Cognitive_distortion.

16. "Quote Details: Helen Keller: When one door of... - The Quotations Page," Quotes and Famous Sayings - The Quotations Page, accessed April 9, 2011, http://www.quotationspage.com/quote/30190.html.

40. Decision-Making 101

1. "Myers-Briggs Type Indicator," Wikipedia, accessed May 5, 2010, http://en.wikipedia.org/wiki/Myers-Briggs.

2. Jonah Lehrer, How We Decide, Kindle ed., (Boston: Houghton Mifflin Harcourt, 2009).

3. "Eric Nehrlich, Unrepentant Generalist || How We Decide, by Jonah Lehrer || April || 2010," Eric Nehrlich, accessed May 5, 2010, http://www.nehrlich.com/blog/2010/04/01/how-we-decide-by-jonah-lehrer/.

41. First Day of May

1. James Taylor, vocal performance of "First of May," by James Taylor, produced by Don Grolnick, released January, 1988, original recording remastered April 25, 2000, on Never Die Young, Columbia/Legacy, 7661849, compact disc.

2. James Taylor, vocal performance of "First of May," by James Taylor, produced by Don Grolnick, released January, 1988, original recording remastered April 25, 2000, on Never Die Young, Columbia/Legacy, 7661849, compact disc.

3. James Taylor, vocal performance of "First of May," by James Taylor, produced by Don Grolnick, released January, 1988, original recording remastered April 25, 2000, on Never Die Young, Columbia/Legacy, 7661849, compact disc.

42. "Senioritis" And What to Do about It

1. "Jean Piaget," NNDB: Tracking the Entire World, accessed February 21, 2010, http://www.nndb.com/people/359/000094077/.

2. Laura Scribner Kastner and Jennifer Fugett Wyatt. The Launching Years: Strategies for Parenting from Senior Year to College Life, (New York: Three Rivers Press, 2002.)

3. Scribner et al, Launching, 47.

4. Scribner et al, Launching, 48.

5. Scribner et al, Launching, 48-49.

6. Scribner et al, Launching, 49-50.

7. Scribner et al, Launching, 50.

8. Scribner et al, Launching, 50.

9. Scribner et al, Launching, 51.

43. No Guts, No Glory

1. Sharon Jayson, "Is this the next baby boom? - USATODAY. com," News, Travel, Weather, Entertainment, Sports, Technology, U.S. & World - USATODAY.com, accessed June 26, 2010, http://www.usatoday.com/news/nation/2008-07-16-baby-boomlet_N.htm.

2. "YouTube - Suzy Bogguss - Letting Go," YouTube - Broadcast Yourself, accessed June 26, 2010, http://www.youtube.com/watch?v=aLyGae5mYoo.

3. Phil Vassar, vocal performance of "She's on Her Way," by Phil Vassar, Tim Nichols, and Jeff Outlaw, produced by Phil Vassar, released December 15, 2009, on Traveling Circus, Universal South, 8054966, compact disc.

46. The Hero's Journey

1. Joseph Campbell, The Hero with a Thousand Faces, 2nd ed., (Princeton, N.J.: Princeton University Press, 1968), 30/ 3rd ed., (California: Novato, 2008), 23.

2. Star Wars: Return of the Jedi, Directed by George Lucas, (Tucson: 20th Century Fox), 2004, DVD.

3. Christopher Vogler, The Writers Journey: Mythic Structure for Writers, 3rd Edition, (Studio City, CA: Michael Wiese Productions, 2007).

4. Judith Viorst, Necessary Losses: the Loves, Illusions, Dependencies, and Impossible Expectations that All of Us Have to Give Up in Order to Grow, (New York: Free Press, 2002).

5. Cat Stevens, vocal performance of "Father and Son," by Cat Stevens, produced by Paul Samwell-Smith recorded July, 1970, released November 23, 1970, original recording remastered 2000, on Tea for the Tillerman, A&M Records, Inc., 1094893, compact disc.

47. Letting Go

1. Barbara K. Hofer and Abigail Sullivan Moore, The iConnected Parent: Staying Close to Your Kids in College (and Beyond) While Letting Them Grow Up, (New York, NY: Free Press, 2010).

2. "Charting Your Course - Career Development - Alumni - Harvard Business School," Alumni - Harvard Business School, accessed August 26, 2009, http://www.alumni.hbs.edu/careers/cyc.html.

3. Suzy Bogguss, vocal performance of "Letting Go," by Doug Crider and Matt Rollings, produced by Suzy Bogguss and Jimmy Bowen, released August 27, 1991, on Aces, Liberty, 1109146, compact disc.

4. Cat Stevens, vocal performance of "Father and Son," by Cat Stevens, produced by Paul Samwell-Smith recorded July, 1970, released November 23, 1970, original recording remastered 2000, on Tea for the Tillerman, A&M Records, Inc., 1094893, compact disc.

5. Phil Vassar, vocal performance of "She's on Her Way," by Phil Vassar, Tim Nichols, and Jeff Outlaw, produced by Phil Vassar, released December 15, 2009, on Traveling Circus, Universal South, 8054966, compact disc.

6. Lee Ann Womack, vocal performance of "I Hope You Dance," by Tia Sillers and Mark D. Sanders, produced by Mark Wright, released May 23, 2000, on I Hope You Dance, MCA Nashville, 1250187, compact disc.

7. John Mellencamp, vocal performance of "Your Life Is Now," by John Mellencamp, produced by John Mellencamp, released October 6, 1998, on John Mellencamp, Columbia Records, 1090455, compact disc.

8. Idina Menzel and Kristin Chenoweth, vocal performance of "For Good," by Stephen Schwartz, produced by Stephen Schwartz, recorded November 10, 2003, released December 16, 2003, on Wicked 2003 Original Broadway Cast, Decca Broadway, 1814594, compact disc.

9. Dixie Chicks, vocal performance of "Wide Open Spaces," by Susan Gibson, produced by Blake Chancey and Paul Worley, released January 27, 1998, on Wide Open Spaces, Monument, 1240816, compact disc.

10. Karen Levin Coburn and Madge Lawrence Treeger, Letting Go: A Parents' Guide to Understanding the College Years, 5th ed. (New York: Harper, 2009).

11. Helen E. Johnson and Christine Miller, Don't Tell Me What to Do, Just Send Money: the Essential Parenting Guide for the College Years, (New York: St. Martin's Griffin, 2000).

12. Patricia Pasick, Almost Grown: Launching Your Child from High School to College, (New York: W.W. Norton, 1998).

13. Cal Newport, How to Become a Straight-A Student: The Unconventional Strategies Real College Students Use to Score High While Studying Less, (New York: Broadway Books, 2007).

14. Harlan Cohen, The Naked Roommate: And 107 Other Issues You Might Run Into in College, 3rd ed. (Naperville, Ill.: Sourcebooks, 2009).

15. Harlan Cohen, The Happiest Kid on Campus: A Parent's Guide to the Very Best College Experience (for You and Your Child), (Naperville, Ill.: Sourcebooks, 2010).

16. Barbara Rainey and Susan Alexander Yates, Barbara & Susan's Guide to the Empty Nest: Discovering New Purpose, Passion & Your Next Great Adventure, (Little Rock, AR: FamilyLife Publishing, 2008).

17. Carol Fishman Cohen and Vivian Steir Rabin, Back on the Career Track: A Guide for Stay-at-Home Moms Who Want to Return to Work, (New York: Business Plus, 2008).

18. "iRelaunch - Career Re-entry Experts - Women Re-entering the Workforce," iRelaunch - Career Re-entry Experts - Women Re-entering the Workforce, accessed August 26, 2009, http://www.irelaunch.com/.

19. James Hollis, Finding Meaning in the Second Half of Life, (New York: Gotham Books, 2006).

49. Helicopter Parents: College and Beyond

1. Jeremy S. Hyman and Lynn F. Jacobs, "10 Reasons Parents Should Never Contact College Professors - Professors' Guide (usnews.com)," US News & World Report | News & Rankings | Best Colleges, Best Hospitals, and more, accessed August 23, 2010, http://www.usnews.com/education/blogs/professors-guide/2010/05/12/10-reasons-parents-should-never-contact-college-professors.html.

2. Rachel Rettner. "'Helicopter' Parents Have Neurotic Kids, Study Suggests | LiveScience," Current News on Space, Animals, Technology, Health, Environment, Culture and History | LiveScience, accessed August 23, 2010, http://www.livescience.com/culture/helicopter-parenting-100603.html.

3. Barbara K. Hofer and Abigail Sullivan Moore, The iConnected Parent: Staying Close to Your Kids in College (and Beyond) While Letting Them Grow Up, (New York, NY: Free Press, 2010).

50. Adjusting to College Life: "Friendsickness"

1. "NASPA Journals Database - NASPA Research," NASPA Journals Database - NASPA Research, accessed August 29, 2009, http://journals.naspa.org/.

2. "Friendsickness in the Transition to College: Precollege Predictors and College Adjustment Correlates," ERIC – World's Largest Digital Library of Education Literature, accessed

August 29, 2009, http://www.eric.ed.gov/ERICWebPortal/search/detailmini.jsp?_nfpb=true&_&ERICExtSearch_SearchValue_0=EJ622721&ERICExtSearch_SearchType_0=no&accno=EJ622721.

3. "NASPA Journals Database - NASPA Research," NASPA Journals Database - NASPA Research, accessed August 29, 2009, http://journals.naspa.org/.

4. "NASPA Journals Database - NASPA Research," NASPA Journals Database - NASPA Research, accessed August 29, 2009, http://journals.naspa.org/.

5. "NASPA Journals Database - NASPA Research," NASPA Journals Database - NASPA Research, accessed August 29, 2009, http://journals.naspa.org/.

6. "Urban Dictionary: sexile," Urban Dictionary, August 29: going ham, accessed August 29, 2009, http://www.urbandictionary.com/define.php?term=sexile.

7. "NASPA Journals Database - NASPA Research," NASPA Journals Database - NASPA Research, accessed August 29, 2009, http://journals.naspa.org/.

51. When Big Brother or Sister Goes to College

1. Helen E. Johnson and Christine Miller, Don't Tell Me What to Do, Just Send Money: the Essential Parenting Guide for the College Years, (New York: St. Martin's Griffin, 2000).

2. Patricia Pasick, Almost Grown: Launching Your Child from High School to College, (New York: W.W. Norton, 1998).

52. College Weekends: Forever Jung

1. "Liminality - Wikipedia, the Free Encyclopedia," Wikipedia, the Free Encyclopedia, accessed October 3, 2010, http://en.wikipedia.org/wiki/Liminality.

2. "Arnold van Gennep - Wikipedia, the Free Encyclopedia," Wikipedia, the Free Encyclopedia, accessed October 3, 2010, http://en.wikipedia.org/wiki/Arnold_van_Gennep.

3. "Victor Turner - Wikipedia, the Free Encyclopedia," Wikipedia, the Free Encyclopedia, accessed October 3, 2010, http://en.wikipedia.org/wiki/Victor_Turner.

4. "Individuation - Wikipedia, the Free Encyclopedia," Wikipedia, the Free Encyclopedia, accessed October 3, 2010, http://en.wikipedia.org/wiki/Individuation.

5. Bani Shorter, An Image Darkly Forming: Women and Initiation, (London: Routledge & Kegan Paul, 1987).

6. Loren Pope, Colleges That Change Lives: 40 Schools That Will Change the Way You Think About Colleges, (New York: Penguin Books, 2006).

7. "Yoda - Wikipedia, the Free Encyclopedia," Wikipedia, the Free Encyclopedia, accessed October 3, 2010, http://en.wikipedia.org/wiki/Yoda.

8. James Hollis, Finding Meaning in the Second Half of Life, (New York: Gotham Books, 2006).

53. College Freshmen Home for Thanksgiving

1. Brianna, Fordham University, " Welcome Home, Honey! : College Candy," College Candy, accessed February 1, 2011, http://collegecandy.com/2009/11/15/welcome-home-honey/.

2. Nicole L Mihalopoulos, Peggy Auinger, and Jonathan Klein. "The Freshman 15: Is it Real?," National Center for Biotechnology Information, accessed February 1, 2011,

3. Richard Kadison and Theresa Foy DiGeronimo, College of the Overwhelmed the Campus Mental Health Crisis and What We Must Do About It, (San Francisco, Calif.: Jossey-Bass, 2005).

4. Barrett Seaman, Binge: What Your College Student Won't Tell You: Campus Life in an Age of Disconnection and Excess, (Hoboken, N.J.: John Wiley & Sons, 2005).

5. Tamar Lewin, "College Freshmen Stress Levels High, Survey Finds - NYTimes.com," The New York Times - Breaking News, World News & Multimedia, accessed February 1, 2011.,

6. William Damon, The Path to Purpose: How Young People Find Their Calling in Life, (New York: Free Press, 2009).

7. Race to Nowhere, Directed by Vicki H. Abeles, (Lafayette, CA: Reel Link Films), 2010, DVD.

8. "College Transfers - About.com: College Admissions," College Admissions, accessed February 1, 2011, http://college-apps.about.com/lr/college_transfers/299478/1/

9. Homeward Bound - The Incredible Journey, Directed by Duwayne Dunham, (Hollywood, CA: Walt Disney Video), 1993, DVD.

VIII. Works Cited

"ACT-SAT Concordance." ACT | Helping People Achieve Education and Workplace Success. http://www.act.org/aap/concordance/ (accessed November 7, 2010).

"About ACT | ACT Company Profile | ACT." ACT | Helping People Achieve Education and Workplace Success. http://www.act.org/aboutact/profile.html (accessed November 7, 2010).

"About Us - The College Board." About Us - The College Board. http://about.collegeboard.org/ (accessed November 7, 2010).

Altman, Alex. "A Brief History Of: Summer Vacation - TIME." Breaking News, Analysis, Politics, Blogs, News Photos, Video, Tech Reviews - TIME.com. http://www.time.com/time/magazine/article/0,9171,1816501,00.html (accessed May 20, 2009).

Antonoff, Steven R. *College Match: A Blueprint for Choosing the Best School for You!*. 5th ed. Alexandria, VA: Octameron Associates, 1997.

Antonoff, Steven R. *The College Finder: Choose the School That's Right for You!*. 3rd ed. Westford, MA: Wintergreen Orchard House, 2008.

"Arnold van Gennep - Wikipedia, the Free Encyclopedia." Wikipedia, the Free Encyclopedia. http://en.wikipedia.org/wiki/Arnold_van_Gennep (accessed October 3, 2010).

Arum, Richard, and Josipa Roksa. *Academically Adrift Limited Learning on College Campuses*. Chicago: University Of Chicago Press, 2011.

Balaban, Mariah, and Jennifer Shields. *Study Away: The Unauthorized Guide to College Abroad*. New York: Anchor Books, 2003.

Bauerlein, Mark. "Teen Narcissism - Brainstorm - The Chronicle of Higher Education." Home - The Chronicle of Higher Education. http://chronicle.com/blogs/brainstorm/teen-narcissism/6535 (accessed April 9, 2011).

Berger, Sandra L.. *The Ultimate Guide to Summer Opportunities for Teens: 200 Programs That Prepare You for College Success*. Waco, Tex.: Prufrock Press, 2008.

"Best Colleges | Find the Best College for You | US News Education." US News & World Report | News & Rankings | Best Colleges, Best Hospitals, and more. http://colleges.usnews.rankingsandreviews.com/best-colleges (accessed March 5, 2011).

"Best Values in Public Colleges, 2010-11." Kiplinger - Personal Finance, Business, Investing, Retirement, and Financial Advice. http://www.kiplinger.com/tools/colleges/ (accessed March 5, 2011).

"Binghamton University - Admission: Undergraduate Admission: Costs and Financial Aid: Affording Binghamton." Binghamton University - Home. http://www2.binghamton.edu/admissions/attendance-costs.html (accessed March 5, 2011).

"Broadreach Teen Summer Camps. Scuba Camps, Caribbean Sailing Camps, Marine Biology, Teen Travel, Wilderness Summer Programs." Broadreach Teen Summer Camps. Scuba Camps, Caribbean Sailing Camps, Marine Biology, Teen Travel, Wilderness Summer Programs. http://www.gobroadreach.com/ (accessed May 20, 2009).

Brokaw, Tom. *The Greatest Generation* . New York: Random House, 1998.

Brooks, Ph.D., Robert. "Education and "Charismatic" Adults: To Touch a StudentÂ's Heart and Mind." Psychologist, Motivational Speaker, and Author on Resilience, Motivation, and Family Relationships: Dr. Robert Brooks. http://www.drrobertbrooks.com/writings/articles/0009.html (accessed January 28, 2011).

Brooks, Ph.D., Robert, and Sam Goldstein, Ph.D.. *Raising Resilient Children: Fostering Strength, Hope, and Optimism, in Your Child.* Chicago: Contemporary Books, 2001.

Buchmann, Claudia, Vincent Roscigno, and Dennis Condron. "(Page 1 of 23) - The Myth of Meritocracy? SAT Preparation, College Enrollment, Class and Race in the United States authored by Buchmann, Claudia., Roscigno, Vincent. and Condron, Dennis." All Academic Inc. (Abstract Management, Conference Management and Research Search Engine). http://www.allacademic.com//meta/p_mla_apa_research_citation/1/0/4/5/5/pages104558/p104558-1.php (accessed November 9, 2010).

Campbell, Joseph. *The Hero with a Thousand Faces* . 2nd ed. Princeton, N.J.: Princeton University Press, 1968.

Campbell, Joseph. *The Hero with a Thousand Faces* . 3rd ed. California: Novato, 2008.

"Charting Your Course - Career Development - Alumni - Harvard Business School." Alumni - Harvard Business School. http://www.alumni.hbs.edu/careers/cyc.html (accessed August 26, 2009).

Chua, Amy. *Battle Hymn of the Tiger Mother.* USA: The Penguin Press, 2011.

City Slickers. DVD. Directed by Ron Underwood. United States: Columbia Pictures, 1991.

"Class Schedule - High School Courses - English, Math, Social Studies." College Admissions - SAT - University & College Search Tool. http://www.collegeboard.com/student/plan/high-school/33.html (accessed August 31, 2009).

Cline, Foster W., and Jim Fay. *Parenting with Love and Logic: Teaching Children Responsibility.* CO: Pinon Press, 1990.

Clinedinst, Melissa, and David Hawkins. "State of College Admission 2010 Report." NACACNet. http://www.nacanet.org/PublicationsResources/marketplace/research/Pages/StateofCollegeAdmission.aspx (accessed January 28, 2011).

Clinton, Hillary Rodham. *It Takes a Village.* New York : Simon & Schuster, 1996.

Coburn, Karen Levin, and Madge Lawrence Treeger. *Letting Go: A Parents' Guide to Understanding the College Years.* 5th ed. New York: Harper, 2009.

"Cognitive Distortion - Wikipedia, the Free Encyclopedia." Wikipedia, the Free Encyclopedia. http://en.wikipedia.org/wiki/Cognitive_distortion (accessed April 9, 2011).

Cohen, Carol Fishman. "In Japan and Korea, Asian-style Parenting Means Mom Stays Home." Working Mother. http://www.workingmother.com/BestCompanies/thought-leaders/2011/01/in-japan-and-korea-asian-style-parenting-means-mom-stays-home (accessed January 28, 2011).

Cohen, Carol Fishman, and Vivian Steir Rabin. *Back on the Career Track: A Guide for Stay-at-Home Moms Who Want to Return to Work.* New York: Business Plus, 2008.

Cohen, Harlan. *The Naked Roommate: And 107 Other Issues You Might Run Into in College.* 3rd ed. Naperville, Ill.: Sourcebooks, 2009.

Cohen, Harlan. *The Happiest Kid on Campus: A Parent's Guide to the Very Best College Experience (for You and Your Child)*. Naperville, Ill.: Sourcebooks, 20&

College Board. *Book of Majors 2011 (College Board Book of Majors)*. New York: College Board Publications, 2011.

"College Compass." US News & World Report College Compass. http://premium.usnews.com/best-colleges (accessed March 5, 2011).

"College Rankings & Scholarships | InsideCollege.com." College Rankings & Scholarships | InsideCollege.com. http://www.insidecollege.com/reno/home.do (accessed October 4, 2010).

"College Rankings & Scholarships | InsideCollege.com." College Rankings & Scholarships | InsideCollege.com. http://www.insidecollege.com/reno/home.do (accessed January 23, 2010).

"College Transfers - About.com : College Admissions." College Admissions. http://collegeapps.about.com/lr/college_transfers/299478/1/ (accessed February 1, 2011).

"Compass SAT Subject Tests FAQ." Compass Education Group. http://www.compassprep.com/subject_faq.shtml#faq19 (accessed November 8, 2010).

"Compass: Admissions Requirements." Compass Education Group. http://www.compassprep.com/admissions_req_subjects.aspx (accessed November 8, 2010).

"Congressional Award: Congress' Award for Youth." Congressional Award: Congress' Award for Youth. http://www.congressionalaward.org/ (accessed May 20, 2009).

Crary, David . "Study Finds Students Narcissistic - Boston.com." Featured Articles From Boston.com. http://articles.boston.

com/2007-02-27/news/29231950_1_college-students-study-(accessed April 9, 2011).

Damon, William. *The Path to Purpose: How Young People Find Their Calling in Life.* New York: Free Press, 2009.

Dead Poets Society (Special Edition). DVD. Directed by Peter Weir. Hartford: Buena Vista Home Entertainment / Touchstone, 1989.

Dunbar, Don, and G. F. Lichtenberg. *What You Don't Know Can Keep You Out of College: A Top Consultant Explains the 13 Fatal Application Mistakes and Why Character Is the Key to College Admissions.* New York, N.Y.: Gotham Books, 2007.

Easterbrook, Gregg. *The Progress Paradox: How Life Gets Better While People Feel Worse.* New York: Random House, 2003.

"Encyclopaedia Britannica - Wikipedia, the Free Encyclopedia." Wikipedia, the Free Encyclopedia. http://en.wikipedia.org/wiki/Encyclop%C3%A6dia_Britannica (accessed March 5, 2011).

"Eric Nehrlich, Unrepentant Generalist ‖ How We Decide, by Jonah Lehrer ‖ April ‖ 2010." Eric Nehrlich. http://www.nehrlich.com/blog/2010/04/01/how-we-decide-by-jonah-lehrer/ (accessed May 5, 2010).

Ericsson, Dr. K. Anders. "Dr. K. Anders Ericsson." Psychology at Florida State University. http://www.psy.fsu.edu/faculty/ericsson.dp.html (accessed November 9, 2010).

"Family Finance Â– Financial Planning, Budgeting, Managing Money - Kiplinger." Kiplinger - Personal Finance, Business, Investing, Retirement, and Financial Advice. http://www.kiplinger.com/family-finance/ (accessed May 6, 2010).

"Famous Quotes by Roseanne Barr | Quotes Daddy." 1,000,000 Famous Quotes and Quotations | QuotesDaddy. http://www.

quotesdaddy.com/author/Roseanne+Barr (accessed January 13, 2011).

"Fastweb : Scholarships, Financial Aid, Student Loans and Colleges." Fastweb : Scholarships, Financial Aid, Student Loans and Colleges. http://www.fastweb.com/ (accessed May 6, 2010).

"FinAid! Financial Aid, College Scholarships and Student Loans." FinAid! Financial Aid, College Scholarships and Student Loans. http://www.finaid.org/ (accessed May 6, 2010).

Foderaro, Lisa W. "The Whole Applicant - NYTimes. com." The New York Times - Breaking News, World News & Multimedia. http://www.nytimes. com/2009/11/01/education/edlife/01admission-t. html?_r=1&adxnnl=1&adxnnlx=1283861020-1LP8gB-kyjQX1GLp0C635Mw (accessed January 30, 2011).

Fordham University, Brianna. " Welcome Home, Honey! : College Candy." College Candy. http://collegecandy.com/2009/11/15/welcome-home-honey/ (accessed February 1, 2011).

"Friendsickness in the Transition to College: Precollege Predictors and College Adjustment Correlates." ERIC â€" Worldâ€™s Largest Digital Library of Education Literature. http://www.eric.ed.gov/ERICWebPortal/search/detailmini.jsp?_nfpb=true&_&ERICExtSearch_SearchValue_0=EJ622721&ERICExtSearch_SearchType_0=no&accno=EJ622721 (accessed August 29, 2009).

"GS Central: Girl Scout Gold Award." Girl Scouts of the USA: Official Web Site. http://www.girlscouts.org/program/gs_central/insignia/highest_awards/gold_award.asp (accessed May 20, 2009).

Gabriel, Trip. "The Almighty Essay Is a Tough Assignment - NYTimes.com." The New York Times - Breaking News, World News & Multimedia. http://www.nytimes.com/2011/01/09/

education/09guidance-t.html? r=1 (accessed January 30, 2011).

Greene, Howard , and Matthew W. Greene. *The Hidden Ivies, 2nd Edition: 50 Top Colleges - from Amherst to Williams - That Rival the Ivy League* . New York: Harper Collins Publishers, 2009.

"Habitat for Humanity Int'l." Habitat for Humanity Int'l. http://www.habitat.org/ (accessed May 20, 2009).

Heinlein, Robert A.. *Time Enough for Love*. New York: Putnam, 1973.

A Is for Admission: The Insider's Guide to Getting Into the Ivy League and Other Top Colleges. New York: Warner Books, 1997.

Higgins, Tim. *Pay for College Without Sacrificing Your Retirement: A Guide to Your Financial Future*. Point Richmond, California: Bay Tree Publishing, 2008.

"Higher Education Research Institute (HERI) - HERI Home." Higher Education Research Institute (HERI) - HERI Home. http://www.heri.ucla.edu/index.php (accessed February 5, 2011).

Hillman, James. *The Soul's Code: In Search of Character and Calling*. New York: Random House, 1996.

Hintz, Kris. "NJ College Admissions Consultant & Coach, NJ College Advisor, College Admissions Coach New Jersey Â– Position U 4 College ." NJ College Admissions Consultant & Coach, NJ College Advisor, College Admissions Coach New Jersey Â– Position U 4 College . http://www.positionu4college.com/ (accessed January 27, 2011).

Hintz, Kris. "Careerblog by Kris Hintz." Careerblog by Kris Hintz. http://positionu4life.wordpress.com/ (accessed February 10, 2011).

Hintz, Kris. "Collegeblog by Kris Hintz." Collegeblog by Kris Hintz. http://positionu4college.wordpress.com/ (accessed January 27, 2011).

Hofer, Barbara K., and Abigail Sullivan Moore. *The iConnected Parent: Staying Close to Your Kids in College (and Beyond) While Letting Them Grow Up*. New York, NY: Free Press, 2010.

Hollis, James. *Finding Meaning in the Second Half of Life* . New York: Gotham Books, 2006.

Homeward Bound - The Incredible Journey. DVD. Directed by Duwayne Dunham. Hollywood, CA: Walt Disney Video, 1993.

Hyman, Jeremy S., and Lynn F. Jacobs. "10 Reasons Parents Should Never Contact College Professors - Professors' Guide (usnews.com)." US News & World Report | News & Rankings | Best Colleges, Best Hospitals, and more. http://www.usnews. com/education/blogs/professors-guide/2010/05/12/10-reasons-parents-should-never-contact-college-professors.html (accessed August 23, 2010).

"Individuation - Wikipedia, the Free Encyclopedia." Wikipedia, the Free Encyclopedia. http://en.wikipedia.org/wiki/Individuation (accessed October 3, 2010).

"Iroise Dumontheil | Karolinska Institute - Academia.edu ." Karolinska Institute - Academia.edu . http://ki.academia.edu/IroiseDumontheil (accessed April 9, 2011).

Jayson, Sharon. "Is this the next baby boom? - USATODAY.com." News, Travel, Weather, Entertainment, Sports, Technology, U.S. & World - USATODAY.com. http://www.usatoday.com/news/nation/2008-07-16-baby-boomlet_N.htm (accessed June 26, 2010).

"Jean Piaget." NNDB: Tracking the Entire World. http://www.nndb. com/people/359/000094077/ (accessed February 21, 2010).

"Jean Piaget - Wikipedia, the Free Encyclopedia." Wikipedia, the Free Encyclopedia. http://en.wikipedia.org/wiki/Jean_Piaget (accessed April 9, 2011).

Johnson, Helen E., and Christine Miller. *Don't Tell Me What to Do, Just Send Money: the Essential Parenting Guide for the College Years.* New York: St. Martin's Griffin, 2000.

Kadison, Richard, and Theresa Foy DiGeronimo. *College of the Overwhelmed the Campus Mental Health Crisis and What We Must Do About It.* San Francisco, Calif.: Jossey-Bass, 2005.

Kaplan, Benjamin R.. *How to Go to College Almost for Free: The Secrets of Winning Scholarship Money.* 2nd ed. New York: Harper Resource, 2002.

Kastner, Laura Scribner, and Jennifer Fugett Wyatt. *The Launching Years: Strategies for Parenting from Senior Year to College Life.* new york: Three Rivers Press, 2002.

Keegan, Edward. "The Top 10 U.S. Undergraduate Degree Programs in Architecture - Students, Education, Architecture - Architect Magazine." Architect Magazine: Architectural Design | Architect Online: A premier site for Architecture Industry News & Building Resources. http://www.architect-magazine.com/architecture/the-undergraduate-programs.aspx (accessed January 23, 2010).

Keller, George. *Transforming a College: The Story of a Little Known College's Strategic Climb to National Distinction.* Baltimore: The Johns Hopkins University Press, 2004.

"LeadAmerica Youth Leadership Programs | Academic Summer Programs for High School Students | College Readiness." LeadAmerica Youth Leadership Programs | Academic Summer Programs for High School Students | College Readiness. http://www.lead-america.org/ (accessed May 20, 2009).

Lehrer, Jonah. *How We Decide*. Kindle ed. Boston: Houghton Mifflin Harcourt, 2009.

Levine, Madeline. *The Price of Privilege: How Parental Pressure and Material Advantage Are Creating a Generation of Disconnected and Unhappy Kids*. New York: HarperCollins, 2006.

Lewin, Tamar. "College Freshmen Stress Levels High, Survey Finds - NYTimes.com." The New York Times - Breaking News, World News & Multimedia. http://www.nytimes.com/2011/01/27/education/27colleges.html?_r=1 (accessed February 1, 2011).

Lewin, Tamar. "College Freshmen Stress Levels High, Survey Finds - NYTimes.com." The New York Times - Breaking News, World News & Multimedia. http://www.nytimes.com/2011/01/27/education/27colleges.html?_r=1 (accessed February 5, 2011).

"Liberal Arts - Wikipedia, the Free Encyclopedia." Wikipedia, the Free Encyclopedia. http://en.wikipedia.org/wiki/Liberal_arts (accessed March 5, 2011).

"Liminality - Wikipedia, the Free Encyclopedia." Wikipedia, the Free Encyclopedia. http://en.wikipedia.org/wiki/Liminality (accessed October 3, 2010).

"Little Kids Rock." Little Kids Rock. http://littlekidsrock.org/what-we-do.html (accessed February 23, 2011).

Loveland, Elaina. *Creative Colleges: A Guide for Student Actors, Artists, Dancers, Musicians and Writers*. Belmont, CA: SuperCollege, LLC, 2005.

"Magical Thinking - Wikipedia, the Free Encyclopedia." Wikipedia, the Free Encyclopedia. http://en.wikipedia.org/wiki/Magical_thinking (accessed April 9, 2011).

"Marketplace." NACAC Homepage. http://www.nacacnet.org/PublicationsResources/Marketplace/Pages/default.aspx (accessed June 7, 2010).

"MeritAid.com: Search Merit Scholarships, Academic Scholarships, Merit Awards - Merit Aid - Search." MeritAid.com: Search Merit Scholarships, Academic Scholarships, Merit Awards - Merit Aid - Search. http://www.meritaid.com/ (accessed May 6, 2010).

Mihalopoulos, Nicole L., Peggy Auinger, and Jonathan Klein. "The Freshman 15: Is it Real?." National Center for Biotechnology Information. http://www.ncbi.nlm.nih.gov/pmc/articles/PMC2532948/ (accessed February 1, 2011).

"Myers-Briggs Type Indicator." Wikipedia. http://en.wikipedia.org/wiki/Myers-Briggs (accessed May 5, 2010).

"NASPA Journals Database - NASPA Research." NASPA Journals Database - NASPA Research. http://journals.naspa.org/ (accessed August 29, 2009).

"National Honor Society and National Junior Honor Society - NHS & NJHS." National Honor Society and National Junior Honor Society - NHS & NJHS. http://www.nhs.us/ (accessed May 20, 2009).

"National Merit Scholarship Corporation." National Merit Scholarship Corporation. http://www.nationalmerit.org/index.php (accessed August 6, 2009).

"National Merit Scholarship Corporation - NMSP." National Merit Scholarship Corporation. http://www.nationalmerit.org/nmsp.php (accessed November 8, 2010).

"Naviance - The Leading Provider of K-12 Solutions that Inspire Students to Achieve Post-Secondary Success." Naviance -The Leading Provider of K-12 Solutions that Inspire Students to Achieve Post-Secondary Success. http://www.naviance.com/ (accessed December 1, 2009).

Newport, Cal. *How to Become a Straight-A Student: The Unconventional Strategies Real College Students Use to Score High While Studying Less.* New York: Broadway Books, 2007.

"Number of Educational Institutions, by Level and Control of Institution: Selected Years, 1980â€"81 through 2004â€"05." National Center for Education Statistics (NCES) Home Page, a part of the U.S. Department of Education. http://nces.ed.gov/programs/digest/d06/tables/dt06_005.asp (accessed December 26, 2010).

O'Shaughnessy, Lynn. "The College Solution Blog." The College Solution Blog. http://www.thecollegesolutionblog.com/ (accessed August 31, 2009).

O'Shaughnessy, Lynn. *The College Solution: A Guide for Everyone Looking for the Right School at the Right Price.* NJ: FT Press, 2008.

Onwuegbuzie, Anthony J. , and Michael A. Seaman. "The Effect of Time Constraints and Statistics Test Anxiety on Test Performance in a Statistics Course by Anthony J. Onwuegbuzie." Questia - The Online Library of Books and Journals. http://www.questia.com/read/98487204?title=The%20Effect%20of%20Time%20Constraints%20and%20Statistics%20Test%20Anxiety%20on%20Test%20Performance%20in%20a%20Statistics%20Course (accessed December 26, 2010).

"Optional List | FairTest." The National Center for Fair & Open Testing | FairTest. http://www.fairtest.org/university/optional (accessed November 8, 2010).

Pasick, Patricia. *Almost Grown: Launching Your Child from High School to College.* New York: W.W. Norton, 1998.

Pope, Loren. *Colleges That Change Lives: 40 Schools That Will Change the Way You Think About Colleges.* New York: Penguin Books, 2006.

"Public University - Wikipedia, the Free Encyclopedia." Wikipedia, the Free Encyclopedia. http://en.wikipedia.org/wiki/Public_university (accessed March 5, 2011).

"Quote Details: Helen Keller: When one door of... - The Quotations Page." Quotes and Famous Sayings - The Quotations Page. http://www.quotationspage.com/quote/30190.html (accessed April 9, 2011).

Race to Nowhere. DVD. Directed by Vicki H. Abeles. Lafayette, CA: Reel Link Films, 2010.

"Race to Nowhere | About the Film." Race to Nowhere | Changing Lives One Film at a Time. http://www.racetonowhere.com/about-film (accessed February 5, 2011).

Rainey, Barbara, and Susan Alexander Yates. *Barbara & Susan's Guide to the Empty Nest: Discovering New Purpose, Passion & Your Next Great Adventure*. Little Rock, AR: FamilyLife Publishing, 2008.

"Research & Statistics - ED.gov." U.S. Department of Education. http://ed.gov/rschstat/landing.jhtml (accessed June 7, 2010).

Rettner, Rachel. " 'Helicopter' Parents Have Neurotic Kids, Study Suggests | LiveScience ." Current News on Space, Animals, Technology, Health, Environment, Culture and History | LiveScience . http://www.livescience.com/culture/helicopter-parenting-100603.html (accessed August 23, 2010).

"Ryan's Well Foundation | About Us." Ryan's Well Foundation | Home. http://www.ryanswell.ca/about-us.aspx (accessed February 23, 2011).

"SAT Percentile Ranks, 2010 College-Bound Seniors Critical Reading, Mathematics, and Writing Percentile Ranks." College Board . http://professionals.collegeboard.com/profdownload/sat-percentile-ranks-2010.pdf (accessed November 8, 2010).

Sandberg, Jared. " Explaining 'VP, Biz Dev' to Your Kid - The Juggle - WSJ." WSJ Blogs - WSJ. http://blogs.wsj.com/juggle/2007/07/11/explaining-vp-biz-dev-to-your-kid/ (accessed February 23, 2011).

Schoenberg, Edward, and Kavin Buck. *A Guide to College Choices for the Performing and Visual Arts* . Raleigh, NC: Lulu.com, 2008.

Schworm, Peter. "Colleges Favoring Applicants Who Show Keen Interest - The Boston Globe." Boston.com. http://www.boston.com/news/education/higher/articles/2009/03/15/a new factor in making that college loving it/ (accessed June 15, 2010).

Seaman, Barrett. *Binge: What Your College Student Won't Tell You : Campus Life in an Age of Disconnection and Excess.* Hoboken, N.J.: John Wiley & Sons, 2005.

Shorter, Bani. *An Image Darkly Forming: Women and Initiation.* London: Routledge & Kegan Paul, 1987.

"Social Rejection - Wikipedia, the Free Encyclopedia." Wikipedia, the Free Encyclopedia. http://en.wikipedia.org/wiki/Social rejection (accessed April 9, 2011).

Springer, Sally P., Jon Reider, and Marion R. Franck. *Admission Matters: What Students and Parents Need to Know About Getting into College, Mobipocket Edition..* San Francisco, CA: Jossey-Bass, 2009.

Star Wars: Return of the Jedi. DVD. Directed by George Lucas. Tucson: 20th Century Fox, 2004.

Steinberg, Jacques. "Top Colleges Have Bigger Waiting Lists - NYTimes.com." The New York Times - Breaking News, World News & Multimedia. http://www.nytimes.com/2010/04/14/education/14waitlist.html? r=1 (accessed January 28, 2011).

Steinberg, Jacques. "College Students' Transfer Rate Is About 1 in 3 - NYTimes.com." College Admissions Advice - The Choice Blog - NYTimes.com. http://thechoice.blogs.nytimes.com/2010/04/27/transfer/ (accessed June 15, 2010).

Stevens, Mitchell L.. *Creating a Class: College Admissions and the Education of Elites.* Cambridge, Mass.: Harvard University Press, 2007.

Strauch, Barbara. *The Primal Teen: What the New Discoveries about the Teenage Brain Tell Us about Our Kids.* New York: Doubleday, 2003.

"Study Illuminates the 'Pain' of Social Rejection." Science Daily: News & Articles in Science, Health, Environment & Technology. http://www.sciencedaily.com/releases/2011/03/110328151726.htm (accessed April 9, 2011).

"Swim with the Dolphins at Dolphin Research Center Marathon FL, Dolphin and Sea Lion Research." Swim with the Dolphins at Dolphin Research Center Marathon FL, Dolphin and Sea Lion Research. http://www.dolphins.org/ (accessed February 23, 2011).

"Teen Adventure Travel | Summer Programs Abroad | Adventure Camps for Teens." Teen Adventure Travel | Summer Programs Abroad | Adventure Camps for Teens. http://www.overland-summers.com/ (accessed May 20, 2009).

"The Civil War (TV series) - Wikipedia, the Free Encyclopedia." Wikipedia, the Free Encyclopedia. http://en.wikipedia.org/wiki/The_Civil_War_%28TV_series%29 (accessed January 13, 2011).

"The Civil War . The Film . Music of the Civil War | PBS." PBS: Public Broadcasting Service. http://www.pbs.org/civilwar/film/music.html (accessed January 13, 2011).

"The Civil War . The War . Historical Documents . Sullivan Ballou Letter | PBS." PBS: Public Broadcasting Service. http://www.pbs.org/civilwar/war/ballou_letter.html (accessed January 28, 2011).

"The Common Application." The Common Application. https://www.commonapp.org/CommonApp/default.aspx (accessed October 30, 2010).

The Miracle Worker. DVD. Directed by Arthur Penn. Pittsburgh: MGM (Video & Dvd), 1962.

"Trends, Strategies, Research for Design Professionals : Design-Intelligence." Trends, Strategies, Research for Design Professionals : DesignIntelligence. http://www.di.net/ (accessed January 23, 2010).

Twenge, Jean M., and W. Keith Campbell. The NarcissismEpidemic: Living in the Age of Entitlement. New York: Free Press, 2009.

"Upromise How it Works, Earn Money for College with Everyday Purchases ." Upromise Welcome, Money for College through Shopping Online, eCoupons, Grocery, Restaurants, Upromise Credit Card, $ Finance, Auto, Home, & More. http://www.upromise.com/welcome/how-it-works (accessed May 6, 2010).

"Urban Dictionary: passion." Urban Dictionary, March 4: going ham. http://www.urbandictionary.com/define.php?term=passion (accessed March 4, 2010).

"Urban Dictionary: sexile." Urban Dictionary, August 29: going ham. http://www.urbandictionary.com/define.php?term=sexile (accessed August 29, 2009).

"Victor Turner - Wikipedia, the Free Encyclopedia." Wikipedia, the Free Encyclopedia. http://en.wikipedia.org/wiki/Victor_Turner (accessed October 3, 2010).

"Video Gallery - The Ellen DeGeneres Show." The Ellen DeGeneres Show: The Place for Ellen Tickets, Celebrity Photos, Videos, Games, Giveaways and More. http://ellen.warnerbros.com/videos/?autoplay=true&mediaKey=87584a4b-88d6-4715-85d3-e4c7fe8e8f2d (accessed December 8, 2010).

Viorst, Judith. *Necessary Losses: the Loves, Illusions, Dependencies, and Impossible Expectations that All of Us Have to Give Up in Order to Grow.* New York: Free Press, 2002.

Vise, Daniel de. "College Wait Lists Grow as Schools Hedge Bets on Enrollment Numbers." Washington Post - Politics, National, World & D.C. Area News and Headlines - washingtonpost.com. http://www.washingtonpost.com/wp-dyn/content/article/2010/05/14/AR2010051403691.html (accessed January 28, 2011).

Vogel, Steve. "College Admissions: SAT vs. ACT: Which Test to Take? Learn the Differences Between the Two." Suite101.com: Online Magazine and Writers' Network. http://www.suite101.com/content/college-admissions-sat-vs-act-a35051 (accessed November 7, 2010).

Vogler, Christopher. *The Writers Journey: Mythic Structure for Writers, 3rd Edition.* Studio City, CA: Michael Wiese Productions, 2007.

"Washington Semester American University Washington, DC." Washington Semester American University Home. www.american.edu/washingtonsemester/ (accessed February 23, 2011).

"Welcome to All Things Human!." Welcome to All Things Human!. http://www.allthingshuman.net/index.php? (accessed April 9, 2011).

"Welcome to the Eagle Scout Resource Center at EagleScout.Org!." Welcome to the Eagle Scout Resource Center at EagleScout.Org!. http://www.eaglescout.org/ (accessed May 20, 2009).

"Where There Be Dragons: Summer & Semester Study Abroad Programs for High School & College Students in Asia, Africa & Americas." *Where There Be Dragons: Summer & Semester Study Abroad Programs for High School & College Students in Asia, Africa & Americas.* http://www.wheretherebedragons.com/ (accessed May 20, 2009).

White, Kristin M.. *The Complete Guide to the Gap Year: The Best Things to Do Between High School and College, Mobipocket Edition.*. San Francisco, CA: Jossey-Bass, 2009.

"Winter 2010 Survey of Community College Presidents | The Campus Computing Project." *The Campus Computing Project.* http://www.campuscomputing.net/winter-2010-survey-community-college-presidents (accessed May 6, 2010).

Wolf, Ph.D., Anthony E.. *Get Out of My Life, but First Could You Drive Me and Cheryl to the Mall?: A Parent's Guide to the New Teenager.* First Revised ed. New York: Farrar, Straus, & Giroux Books, 2002.

Yale Daily News Staff. *The Insider's Guide to the Colleges, 2011: Students on Campus Tell You What You Really Want to Know, 37th Edition.* New Haven, CT: The Yale Daily News Publishing Company, 2011.

"Yoda - Wikipedia, the Free Encyclopedia." *Wikipedia, the Free Encyclopedia.* http://en.wikipedia.org/wiki/Yoda (accessed October 3, 2010).

"YouTube - Suzy Bogguss - Letting Go ." *YouTube - Broadcast Yourself .* http://www.youtube.com/watch?v=aLyGae5mYoo (accessed June 26, 2010).

"iRelaunch - Career Re-entry Experts - Women Re-entering the Workforce." *iRelaunch - Career Re-entry Experts - Women Re-entering the Workforce.* http://www.irelaunch.com/ (accessed August 26, 2009)

Made in the USA
Lexington, KY
04 October 2012